Booker T. Washington and Education

Lucent Library of Black History

Booker T. Washington and Education

Lucent Library of Black History

John F. Wukovits

LUCENT BOOKS

A part of Gale, Cengage Learning

GALE
CENGAGE Learning

Detroit • New York • San Francisco • New Haven, Conn • Waterville, Maine • London

GALE
CENGAGE Learning™

LIBRARY OF CONGRESS CATALOGING-IN-PUBLICATION DATA

Wukovits, John F., 1944-
  Booker T. Washington and education / by John F. Wukovits.
     p. cm. — (Lucent library of Black history)
  Includes bibliographical references and index.
  ISBN 978-1-4205-0052-3 (hardcover)
  1. Washington, Booker T., 1856–1915—Juvenile literature. 2. African Americans—Biography—Juvenile literature. 3. Educators—United States—Biography—Juvenile literature. I. Title.
   E185.97.W4 W
   370.92—dc22
   [B]

                                                                    2008010168

Lucent Books
27500 Drake Rd.
Farmington Hills, MI 48331

ISBN-13: 978-1-4205-0052-3
ISBN-10: 1-4205-0052-X

Printed in the United States of America
1 2 3 4 5 6 7 12 11 10 09 08

Contents

Foreword

It has been more than 500 years since Africans were first brought to the New World in shackles, and over 140 years since slavery was formally abolished in the United States. Over 50 years have passed since the fallacy of "separate but equal" was obliterated in the American courts, and some 40 years since the watershed Civil Rights Act of 1965 guaranteed the rights and liberties of all Americans, especially those of color. Over time, these changes have become celebrated landmarks in American history. In the twenty-first century, African American men and women are politicians, judges, diplomats, professors, deans, doctors, artists, athletes, business owners, and home owners. For many, the scars of the past have melted away in the opportunities that have been found in contemporary society. Observers such as Peter N. Kirsanow, who sits on the U.S. Commission of Civil Rights, point to these accomplishments and conclude, "The growing black middle class may be viewed as proof that most of the civil rights battles have been won."

In spite of these legal victories, however, prejudice and inequality have persisted in American society. In 2003, African Americans comprised just 12 percent of the nation's population, yet accounted for 44 percent of its prison inmates and 24 percent of its poor. Racially motivated hate crimes continue to appear on the pages of major newspapers in many American cities. Furthermore, many African Americans still experience either overt or muted racism in their daily lives. A 1996 study undertaken by Professor Nancy Krieger of the Harvard School of Public Health, for example, found that 80 percent of the African American participants reported having experienced racial discrimination in one or more settings, including at work or school, applying for housing and medical care, from the police or in the courts, and on the street or in a public setting.

It is for these reasons that many believe the struggle for racial equality and justice is far from over. These episodes of discrimination threaten to shatter the illusion that America has completely overcome its racist past, causing many black Americans to become increasingly frustrated and confused. Scholar and writer Ellis Cose has described this splintered state in the following way: "I have done everything I was supposed to do. I have stayed out of trouble with the law, gone to the right schools, and worked myself nearly to death. What more do they want? Why in God's name won't they accept me as a full human being?" For Cose and others, the struggle for equality and justice has yet to be fully achieved.

In many subtle yet important ways the traumatic experiences of slavery and segregation continue to inform the way race is discussed and experienced in the twenty-first century. Indeed, it is possible that America will always grapple with the fallout from its distressing past. Ulric Haynes, dean of the Hofstra University School of Business has said, "Perhaps race will always matter, given the historical circumstances under which we came to this country." But studying this past and understanding how it contributes to present-day dialogues about race and history in America is a critical component of contemporary education. To this end, the Lucent Library of Black History offers a thorough look at the experiences that have shaped the black community and the American people as a whole. Annotated bibliographies provide readers with ideas for further research, while fully documented primary and secondary source quotations enhance the text. Each book in the series explores a different episode of black history; together they provide students with a wealth of information as well as launching points for further study and discussion.

Introduction

A Harvard Honor

The road had been hard—nearly impossible during the most trying moments—for the forty-year-old man pondering his life. Yes, many considered him to be one of the leading educators in the nation, a man who inspired others with his actions and whose ideas prodded still more to succeed. At the same time, despite triumphs that would have earned lesser men world renown, more than half the country considered him inferior, not because of outrageous behavior or a criminal act but because of his skin color.

Booker T. Washington had experienced much in the first four turbulent decades of his life. He was born into slavery, then survived the chaotic Civil War and post–Civil War eras by laboring in mines and teaching himself to read. After obtaining an education, he gained fame by starting a school for blacks, not in the more tolerant northern states but in the midst of the Deep South, at Tuskegee, Alabama, where bigotry by southern whites made life cruel and deadly for southern blacks. Due to Washington's willingness to work hard, the institution succeeded, and soon his ideas circulated inside and outside the United States.

His notions were simple—that blacks could best advance by learning skilled trades such as farming and woodcraft and carpentry. Education's main purpose, he believed, was not to focus on irrelevant subjects such as Greek or Latin, but to teach students how to succeed at those crafts that could help provide an adequate living. Once sufficient numbers of blacks became proficient at those trades, their white counterparts, seeing their value to society, would begin to treat them as equals.

At times Washington wondered if he had taken on an insurmountable challenge. Most black citizens supported his philosophy, but many whites failed to budge from intolerance. The letter in his hand seemed to be vindication, however. Coming from Charles W. Eliot, the president of the most esteemed university in the land, Harvard, the May 28, 1896, letter explained that Washington had been awarded an honorary master of arts degree for his efforts in behalf of all citizens, not just his fellow blacks. This was to be the first such degree issued by Harvard to a black American.

Former slave and pioneering educator Booker T. Washington was the first African American to be awarded an honorary master of arts degree from Harvard University.

Washington stared at the letter, gazed across the veranda of his home in Tuskegee toward his wife and children, then back at the letter, which he called "the greatest surprise that ever came to me."[1] Washington, a former uneducated slave, had been asked by the premier educational institution of the day, a university largely run by and for whites, to accept one of its degrees and to deliver a speech on June 24 at Harvard.

The educator was moved by the invitation. He later recalled of the proud moment:

> As I sat upon my veranda, with this letter in my hand, tears came into my eyes. My whole former life—my life as a slave on the plantation, my work in the coal-mine, the times when I was without food and clothing, when I made my bed under a sidewalk, my struggles for an education, the trying days I had had at Tuskegee, days when I did not know where to turn for a dollar to continue the work there, the ostracism and sometimes oppression of my race—all this passed before me and nearly overcame me.[2]

Students attend class at the Tuskegee Institute, which was headed by Washington from 1881 until his death in 1915.

On June 24 Washington walked into the hall to receive his honor, surrounded by the other gentlemen who would be given similar degrees. General Nelson A. Miles from the U.S. Army, recognized around the country for his leadership fighting the Sioux and Nez Percé tribes out West, walked with Washington. So, too, did Alexander Graham Bell, the creator of the telephone, possibly the most famous of the trio of distinguished guests. As was the Harvard custom, the names of those being honored were kept secret until the ceremony. Upon their introductions, Miles and Bell walked to the podium to polite applause. The assembled students greeted the name of Booker T. Washington, however, with raucous jubilation.

Later, at a dinner during which each man was asked to speak, Washington emphasized his humble beginnings and his gratitude that Harvard had bestowed such an honor on him. He wondered "why you have called me from the Black Belt of the South, from among my humble people, to share in the honors of this occasion"[3] but stated that the award would only prod him to labor harder on behalf of his race. At the conclusion of his words, the audience broke into long and loud applause that dwarfed the reception given to Miles or Bell.

June 24, 1896, was a highlight of Washington's life, but many struggles remained to be fought. As emotional as the day was, and as unaware as he was of what was to come, Washington would soon find himself surrounded by bitter enemies intent on tearing down his efforts. Washington would more easily accept the barbs of white critics and more handily endure the bigotry of his day than the specter of black voices raising doubts about his ideas and leadership. But as always, Washington would bear the condemnation with quiet dignity.

Like the critics who cast doubts upon his life's work, Washington was a product of his times. His ideas and beliefs had been shaped by the slave world in which he grew up. During the tumultuous years following the Civil War, when much of society seemed in transition, he turned to that past to locate principles and actions that could stabilize an uncertain present and bring hope for an improved future.

Chapter One

A Child in Slavery

Because life for slaves on southern plantations was not accurately recorded, Booker T. Washington did not know much about his birth. "I was born a slave on a plantation in Franklin County, Virginia," he writes in his autobiography. "I am not quite sure of the exact place or exact date of my birth, but at any rate I suspect that I must have been born somewhere and at some time."[4] Later research showed that he was born April 5, 1856, but he never learned the name of his father, most likely the white owner of a nearby plantation. His mother, Jane, eventually had three children and married Washington Ferguson, a slave from a neighboring plantation.

Young Booker did not live on a plantation with vast rolling farmland, scores of slaves, a glittering white mansion, and a cruel master, like those pictured in Hollywood movies. Nine members of the Burroughs family, the plantation owners, were crammed into an unspectacular two-story, five-room log house surrounded by a picket fence.

Not far away stood two one-room slave cabins for the ten slaves that worked the fields for James Burroughs and his wife Elizabeth. For the first nine years of his life, Booker lived in a 16- by 14-foot cabin (5m by 4m) that also served as the plantation kitchen. Dominating one end of the structure, a massive fireplace eased the cold wintry nights but kept most slaves out of the sweltering cabin during the humid summers. Cracks in the log walls served as windows. Along with his brother John, Booker slept on a pile of filthy rags placed on the dirt floor.

Like most small plantation owners, James Burroughs scratched out a comfortable but not spectacular living in southwestern Virginia. The ten slaves he owned made him one of the more prosperous gentlemen of the region, but he enjoyed little of the glittering lifestyle enjoyed by major plantation owners. The Burroughs children played with the slave children, and the master and his older sons labored in the fields along with his slaves. No cruel overseer, whip in hand, existed at the Burroughs location.

As a child, Washington lived with his mother and siblings in this cabin on the Virginia plantation of James Burroughs and his family.

Here and there a modest town interrupted the landscape, and a trip to the county seat at Rocky Mount became a major event for white residents starved for entertainment. One local inhabitant stated, "Month after month, year after year, roll by without other things to vary its monotony than the horse-tradings, or public speakings, or private brawls of court days, or an occasional religious revival."[5]

Daily Life

As dreary as life was for white residents, they lived in luxury compared to Booker and the other slaves. His mother cooked over the open fireplace, with pots and skillets hanging above the fire. The simple fare usually consisted of corn and pork for the slaves, while Jane prepared a feast for the Burroughs family. Washington could not recall ever sitting down to a table and eating as a family when he was a boy—when hungry he and every other slave grabbed a piece of bread or meat from the pot and ate on the run.

Occasional treats made life more bearable. Booker loved being given the task of storing sweet potatoes in the deep opening that stood in the center of the dirt floor, as it allowed him the chance to sneak one or two for his enjoyment. On Sunday morning, Booker's mother carefully dished out tiny portions of molasses to the children. To make the treasure seem larger, Booker tilted the plate so the sweet treat spread across the entire surface, then slowly licked the plate clean. One time his mother somehow managed to obtain a chicken, which she cooked as a feast for her children.

Booker was most drawn to the ginger cakes, though, something that was forbidden to him and the other slaves. He recalls watching two of the Burroughs children and their friends enjoying the luxury, an image he turned into a goal. "At that time those cakes seemed to me to be absolutely the most tempting and desirable things that I had ever seen; and I then and there resolved that, if I ever got free, the height of my ambition would be reached if I could get to the point where I could secure and eat ginger-cakes."[6]

Treats, however, did little to ease the trying conditions for Booker. He did not wear his first pair of shoes, even in winter, until he was eight years old, and he walked the fields wearing a single garment—a long harsh flaxen shirt that scratched the skin. "I can scarcely imagine any torture, except, perhaps, the pulling

Entire slave families, including children, were put to work tending to the daily domestic and field chores on the plantation.

of a tooth, that is equal to that caused by putting on a new flax shirt for the first time. It is almost equal to the feeling that one would experience if he had a dozen or more chestnut burrs, or a hundred small pin-points, in contact with his flesh."[7] Booker's brother John often wore the new shirt first to break it in, but nothing completely eliminated the discomfort. Booker had no choice but to wear the garment, which until he was older was the only piece of clothing he was given.

Though James Burroughs treated his slaves well compared to some, he was not above administering punishment when he felt the need. Booker once saw his uncle, a slave named Monroe, tied to a tree, stripped naked, and whipped. As each blow struck his exposed back, Monroe begged, "Pray, master! Pray, master!"[8]

The happiest moments occurred each December, when even the slaves enjoyed a week of celebrations for Christmas. Work stopped, and slaves waited in anticipation for the gifts—mainly simple clothing—the master handed out. One Christmas served as a landmark celebration for Booker. When he crept toward the chimney that morning to see what might fill his stocking, he spotted pieces of red candy and six ginger cakes.

The Hard Life of a Slave

The infrequent happy moments receded before an avalanche of hard work, stifling rules, and dominance by white society. Booker

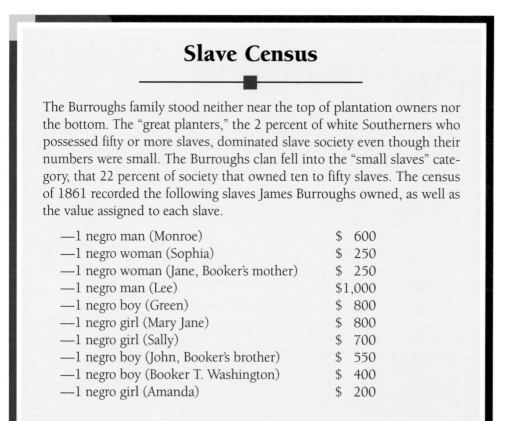

Slave Census

The Burroughs family stood neither near the top of plantation owners nor the bottom. The "great planters," the 2 percent of white Southerners who possessed fifty or more slaves, dominated slave society even though their numbers were small. The Burroughs clan fell into the "small slaves" category, that 22 percent of society that owned ten to fifty slaves. The census of 1861 recorded the following slaves James Burroughs owned, as well as the value assigned to each slave.

—1 negro man (Monroe) $ 600
—1 negro woman (Sophia) $ 250
—1 negro woman (Jane, Booker's mother) $ 250
—1 negro man (Lee) $1,000
—1 negro boy (Green) $ 800
—1 negro girl (Mary Jane) $ 800
—1 negro girl (Sally) $ 700
—1 negro boy (John, Booker's brother) $ 550
—1 negro boy (Booker T. Washington) $ 400
—1 negro girl (Amanda) $ 200

Quoted in Louis R. Harlan, *Booker T. Washington: The Making of a Black Leader, 1856–1901.* New York: Oxford University Press, 1972, p. 8.

could leave the plantation only with a written pass. Even as a young child, he faced a long list of tasks that had to be completed by day's end. He held horses' reins while the Burroughs children mounted for their daily rides, and he operated large fans hanging on ropes and pulleys above the dinner table to help keep flies away from the food and people. Since he was too small to work in the fields with the older male slaves, Booker cleaned the yards around the main house and carried water to the men in the fields. Later in his life, Washington could recall no moment of his childhood when all he had to fret about was play, or even school—work dominated his time.

The chore he most feared, however, was taking the corn to the mill for grinding during the Civil War, which had started in 1861. Each week he had to take a horse, bearing sacks of corn, three miles through the woods to the mill, wait for the grinder to complete the task, and then return to the plantation. Any delay in the process—which often occurred—meant that Booker, no older than seven or eight, would not reach the plantation until well after dark. Sometimes the heavy sacks of corn slipped off the horse, and as Booker was too small to lift the sacks back on, he had to wait along the roadside for a compassionate traveler to stop and help him so he could resume his travel. Booker often stood there, crying in frustration, with sacks of corn lying at his feet.

This situation would bother most young boys, but Booker also heard the rumors that soldiers who had deserted from the Southern army roamed the forests. Rumors swirled that if a slave fell into their hands, they cut off the slave's ears. "The road was a lonely one, and often led through dense forests," Washington writes in his autobiography. "I was always frightened. Besides, when I was late in getting home I knew I would always get a severe scolding or a flogging."[9]

"Getting into Paradise"

As much as the work around the plantation and the fears in the woods bothered Booker, the sight of the Burroughs children heading to school disturbed the youth even more. Each school day the Burroughs boys and girls headed to the one-room structure to learn the basics of reading and writing, but Booker had to

The Emancipation Proclamation

President Abraham Lincoln issued the Emancipation Proclamation on January 1, 1863. The proclamation declared "that all persons held as slaves" within the rebellious states "are, and henceforward shall be free." Since the Emancipation Proclamation applied only to states that had rebelled and left the Union, few slaves were immediately freed. They had to wait until the Union army advanced into their territory and defeated the Confederate army. Only then would the slaves be freed in that region.

The Emancipation Proclamation also announced that African Americans could join the Union army and navy. By the end of the war, almost two hundred thousand black soldiers and sailors had fought for the Union and freedom.

One of the greatest documents in American history, the original Emancipation Proclamation is in the National Archives in Washington, D.C. www.archives.gov/exhibits/featured_documents/emancipation_proclamation.

remain behind to work on the plantation. The wondrous world of education and all the benefits it conveyed—the power of reading and mathematics, the precision of science—existed in a world outside his control. Booker could not grasp why the children he played with could attend school, but he could not.

"We rode together our wooden horses, we fished together in the nearby streams; we played marbles, town-ball, 'tag,' and wrestled together on the parlour floor. And yet, for some reason I did not understand, I was debarred from entering the little schoolhouse with the children of my master."[10]

Booker was like a child staring through the storefront windows at a bright, polished toy he knew he could never possess. He longed to join the Burroughs children, but slavery shut that door of opportunity. Washington says the sight of the Burroughs children heading to school "made a deep impression upon me, and I had the feeling that to get into a schoolhouse and study in this way would be about the same as getting into paradise."[11]

His mother tried to explain that education was for whites and that it was against the law for a slave to learn how to read, but her words only made him more determined to one day attain an education. "I resolved that I should never be satisfied until I learned what this dangerous practice was."[12]

Despite the cruelties of slavery, the Burroughs slaves developed a friendly relationship with their owners. Three Burroughs boys left the farm to fight in the Civil War, and when William Burroughs was killed in action on March 7, 1863, the slaves expressed true sorrow over the loss. Some had nursed "Mars' Billy," as the slaves called him, from childhood. Slave boys had played with him in the fields and had William plead on their behalf to prevent a punishment. "It was no sham sorrow, but real,"[13] Washington writes in his autobiography.

When Benjamin Burroughs returned home with wounds, slaves tended his wounds and watched over him. If all of the Burroughs men had to leave the plantation for some reason, the male slaves competed for the right to sleep in the master's house to protect the Burroughs women. "Anyone attempting to harm 'Young Mistress' or 'Old Mistress' during the night would have had to cross the dead body of the slave to do so,"[14] explains Washington.

Sensing Changes

At the same time, the slaves knew that the outcome of the Civil War carried great importance in their lives. Northern soldiers fought and died, in part, to help free the slaves, so Booker and the other Burroughs slaves followed the war's progress with more than a casual interest. The slave who went to town each week to pick up the mail listened carefully to whites as they chatted about the war, then returned to the plantation to spread the news of a Northern victory or advance. In his autobiography, Washington remembered one night when his mother woke him so that they might pray for freedom.

Booker was not certain what it all meant—war and fighting and above all, freedom—but he knew things seemed to be changing for the better before his eyes. No matter how close they might feel to the Burroughs family, the slaves understood that they existed in an inferior world because their white owners forced them to. Slaves welcomed the opportunity to live their own lives and go where they wanted to go. "I have never seen one [slave] who

The Civil War

—■—

The Civil War split the nation from 1861 to1865 and resulted in 620,000 deaths, more than every other conflict in U.S. history combined. Many factors led to the war. Different ways of life marked the North and South. Most people in the North earned livings based on manufacturing, while the Southern population relied on farming and plantations. The North was willing to hand great power to the federal government in Washington, D.C., while the South favored more powerful state governments and less federal interference. Northern factories flourished with cheap labor, while slavery fueled the operations on Southern plantations.

Slavery overshadowed all other issues, however. Many people in the North felt that slavery was wrong and wanted to abolish the institution. Southern landowners, though, had constructed their farm economy largely on the efforts of cheap slave labor. They were not willing to freely yield such a profitable arrangement.

The bloody four-year war decided the issue. Slavery ended with the Emancipation Proclamation in 1863 and with the victory of Abraham Lincoln's military in April 1865.

did not want to be free, or one who would return to slavery,"[15] he wrote years later.

As the war progressed, Booker noticed that the slaves sang more frequently and with greater feeling than they normally had. It was as if an air of expectancy enveloped the slaves, an expectation that soon, things would be better.

Victorious Northern soldiers were seen more frequently in the adjoining forests and along roadways. They were pursuing the defeated Southern troops as the war drew to a close. At first, the slaves did not know how to react to the sight of Northern soldiers. Were they liberators here to help the slaves? Or were they going to seize the slaves' belongings and harm them?

"The Day of Freedom"

One day the slaves were told to gather at the big house the next morning for an announcement. Few slaves slept much that night, awake with the expectation that tomorrow, "the day of freedom"[16] as Washington calls it, would bring an end to their misery.

The next morning the slaves assembled. The entire Burroughs family either stood or sat on the large porch, accompanied by an official who read from a piece of paper that as of this day the slaves were free people able to go where they wanted and do what they wanted. Booker's mother, with tears running down her cheeks, leaned over, kissed her children, and explained that this was the day she had prayed for all her life.

This depiction of slaves awaiting the stroke of midnight on January 1, 1863, the moment they would be free according to the Emancipation Proclamation, is a scene similar to that experienced by young Washington as the slaves on his plantation anticipated the news of their freedom.

The slaves burst out in celebration. Singing and dancing filled the yard. Booker, barely nine years old, understood that his life would now be different, but as the day stretched into afternoon and evening, he also observed a gradual change in the former slaves.

> I noticed that by the time they returned to their cabins there was a change in their feelings. The great responsibility of being free, of having charge of themselves, of having to think and plan for themselves and their children, seemed to take possession of them. It was very much like suddenly turning a youth of ten or twelve years out into the world to provide for himself.[17]

Freedom had relieved the slaves of one burden yet tossed another their way. Somehow, with little training and less education, they had to scratch out an existence for themselves and their families in a society still dominated by values and laws established by their white masters.

Booker did not yet realize it, but he had just observed events that would help fashion the views and philosophy he would later promote to improve life for blacks in the United States.

Chapter Two

On Fire with One Ambition

Most former slaves speedily abandoned the plantations where they had lived in bondage, but the realities of life in the South gave them little control over their destinies. Everywhere they turned, opportunities to improve were blocked by laws and customs. Denied the chance for an education, the former slaves had little to fall back on to help establish a new life. The few who possessed a skilled trade, such as carpentry, had to compete with whites in a white-dominated society.

Gradually, a steady stream of freedmen returned to what was familiar—the plantation—where they settled into a new arrangement with their former masters. The white landowner permitted the freedmen to till his land in return for a large share of the crops. This new system, called sharecropping, kept blacks in a position of servitude toward the former masters. They were not slaves, but they remained on the land at the mercy of the white landowners. Before blacks could truly be free, someone had to provide a path out of their lowly status.

To Malden
Washington would eventually provide one path, but first he had to escape the squalid conditions that held him back.

Although they were now free, many former slaves returned to plantations to work as sharecroppers, as illustrated by this 1870 depiction of a white farm supervisor and a crew of transient black field hands.

Washington's stepfather, Washington Ferguson, had fled his plantation during the Civil War. He went to Malden, West Virginia, to work in the salt mines. When the war was over, he sent a wagon for his wife and her children so that they could join him. Little did the young Booker know that his stepfather only wanted them in Malden so he could take the little bit of money they would earn working in the salt mines.

In August 1865 Jane and her three children—John, Booker, and Amanda—placed their few belongings in the wagon and started the two-hundred-mile journey to Malden. For weeks the children walked along crude roads and across small streams while Jane, who suffered from asthma and heart palpitations, sat in the wagon. Each night they slept under the stars by a campfire made from tree branches.

As hard as the trip was, life in Malden proved worse. To call the place a town was to elevate its status, for Malden was little more than a collection of squalid shacks, small, garbage-cluttered streets, horrible sanitary conditions, and stench. Fights frequently erupted between drunken workers who spent most of their pay in the numerous saloons. Malden quickly made Booker yearn for the more orderly life that existed with the Burroughs.

His longing deepened when he and his brother John started work at the salt mine. Pumps brought well water to the surface, where large furnaces evaporated the water and left the salt

Many freed slaves, such as those pictured here, left plantation life and settled in cities and towns, where living conditions were usually dirty, cramped, and dangerous.

residue. Miners spread the salt onto large platforms to dry, then other workers packed the salt into barrels for shipping. Booker's job was to pound the salt into the barrels until they weighed 280 pounds (127kg), then mark his barrels with the number "18," indicating it had been packed by him. This simple beginning—the number "18"—was the start of Booker's education. For the first time in his life he recognized what a written symbol meant, and the ability made him yearn for more knowledge.

From as early as 4:00 A.M. until well after dark, Booker labored at the salt mine. It was not unusual for children to be working in those days, and wages as low as fifty cents a day were the norm. Booker, however, could not enjoy even this pittance, which he had to hand over to his stepfather.

An Intense Longing to Read

At least while Booker struggled in the salt mine, he had the example of a fellow black worker who could read. He envied the individual, who, unlike Booker, could learn of distant lands and momentous events by scanning a newspaper or escape the rigors of the mines by immersing himself in a good book.

One of Booker's greatest wishes was to be able to read. "From the time that I can remember having any thoughts about anything," writes Washington in his autobiography, "I recall that I had an intense longing to learn to read. I determined, when quite a small child, that, if I accomplished nothing else in life, I would in some way get enough education to enable me to read common books and newspapers."[18]

All his life, Washington understood the importance of not only setting goals, but overcoming the obstacles blocking one's path toward the goals. He faced one in the guise of his stepfather. Ferguson knew a good thing when he saw one, and he refused to let Booker—and his pay—out of the mine to attend school. Somehow Booker had to find another way to read.

Fortunately, his mother disagreed with Ferguson. She obtained a worn copy of a spelling book, and each night after work Booker opened the volume—the first book he owned—and started to learn the letters of the alphabet. His mother, who could not read a single word, saw how important an education was to her son, so she set her mind to helping him in any way she could.

Richmond Welcome

—◼—

The first time Washington visited Richmond, Virginia, he had to sleep under the city sidewalk. Years later, once he had attained success as a national figure, the black citizens of the city invited Washington to speak before two thousand people. The experience of returning to the scene, this time in triumph, moved Washington to write in his autobiography, "This reception was held not far from the spot where I slept the first night I spent in the city, and I must confess that my mind was more upon the sidewalk that first gave me shelter than upon the reception, agreeable and cordial as it was."

Booker T. Washington, *Up from Slavery*. New York: A.L. Burt, 1900, p. 50.

"Though she was totally ignorant, so far as mere book knowledge was concerned," Washington writes of his mother, "she had high ambitions for her children, and a large fund of good hard, common sense which seemed to enable her to meet and master every situation. If I have done anything in life worth attention, I feel sure that I inherited the disposition from my mother."[19]

A School Opens

Booker's chances for an education improved when William Davis, a black Civil War veteran from Ohio, arrived in Malden and opened a school. Booker badly wanted to attend, but his stepfather continued to refuse permission. Jane arranged for the teacher to visit Booker some nights to instruct him in reading and writing, and the two eventually wore down Ferguson's objections. He allowed Booker to attend school, as long as the boy worked in the salt mine from 4:00 A.M. until 9:00 A.M., as well as after school until dark.

On Booker's first day, he noticed that during roll call, each student gave both his first and last names. Until then, Booker had been called simply "Booker," and when the teacher asked for his name, the startled new student replied impulsively, "Booker Washington." He later stated that he did not know whether he

Organizational Skills

Washington believed that a person had to possess certain qualities in order to succeed. One quality he placed at the top of the list was a sense of organization. It helped him achieve goals and overcome obstacles at each stage of his life.

Now the basis of civilization is system, order, regularity. A race or an individual which has no fixed habits, no time for going to bed, for getting up in the morning, for going to work; no arrangement, order, or system in all the ordinary business of life, such a race and such an individual are lacking in self-control, lacking in some of the fundamentals of civilization.

If you take advantage of all these opportunities, if your minds are so disposed that you can welcome and make the most of these advantages, these habits of order and system will soon be so fixed, so ingrained, so thoroughly a part of you that you will no longer tolerate disorder anywhere.

Quoted in Emmett J. Scott and Lyman Beecher Stowe, *Booker T. Washington: Builder of a Civilization.* Garden City, NY: Doubleday, Page, 1918, p. 231.

thought of the surname Washington after George Washington or after his stepfather, but in any case, he now was known as Booker Washington. Later in life, when his mother explained that she had given him the surname Taliaferro at birth, Washington added that as his middle name.

Booker also noticed that the other schoolchildren wore hats. Since she had no money to purchase a new hat from the local store, his mother sewed together two pieces of cloth, a practical step for the parent but an embarrassing one for the student, who became the butt of classmates' teasing. Rather than being angry with his mother, Booker was proud that she avoided going into debt just to purchase a hat that might impress others. "Since that time I have owned many kinds of caps and hats, but never one of which I have felt so proud as of the cap made by the two pieces of cloth sewed together by my mother,"[20] he later explained. Thrift became a cornerstone quality marking Washington throughout life.

One thing bothered young Booker. Images in his geography book depicted Africans as naked, uncivilized people sporting rings in their noses. That representation clashed with what he saw around him, especially with the example of his mother. He claimed that "a race which could produce as good and gentle and loving a woman as my mother must have some good in it that the geographers had failed to discover," and vowed to "spend my life in helping and strengthening the people of my race, in order to prove to the world that it should learn to respect them in the future, both for what they were and what they should be able to do."[21]

Conditions worsened when the mine owner transferred Booker to the coal mines. Booker hated working one mile below

Although schools serving former slaves, such as the one depicted here, opened after the Civil War, many children, including Washington, were unable to attend on a regular basis because their families needed them to work to earn money.

the surface of the earth, surrounded by coal dust that make all workers, black and white, appear the same color. He feared being crushed to death by a mine collapse or an explosion, which occurred with startling frequency in his time, and the longer schedule forced him to miss much school.

The difficult situation taught Booker a lesson. Still eager to learn, Booker brought a book with him and during breaks read by the light of a miner's lamp. It did not replace school, but it at least kept the academic world in the picture, and it illustrated that he was determined to surmount any hardship placed in his path. "I have learned that success is to be measured not so much by the position that one has reached in life as by the obstacles which he had overcome while trying to succeed,"[22] he states in his autobiography.

"Am I Getting On?"

Fortunately, another individual entered Booker's life at this time. Viola Ruffner, the wife of the mine owner, needed a houseboy to clean her home and run errands. The demanding woman, who insisted that every room sparkle with cleanliness, had already gone through a string of houseboys, none of whom satisfied her rigid demands, but when Booker heard of the opening he quickly applied. He figured that anything had to be better than the mines.

The proper lady from New England and the former slave got off to a rocky start. Ruffner's demands—she always inspected his work to ensure thoroughness—tested Booker's patience. At least a half dozen times the youth quit for other endeavors, including a brief stint as a cabin boy on a steamer ship heading to Cincinnati, Ohio. Always, though, he returned to Ruffner. "He left me half a dozen times to try his hand at different occupations," she explained, "but he always came back to me."[23]

Booker could not leave Ruffner because, in many ways, they were kindred spirits. She emphasized cleanliness, doing things the proper way, never leaving a job until it was finished, the ethic of hard work, thrift, and proper manners and morals—qualities that appealed to the developing young boy. "I soon began to learn that, first of all, she wanted everything kept clean about her, that she wanted things done promptly and systematically, and that at the bottom of everything she wanted absolute honesty and frankness. Nothing must be sloven [messy] or slipshod; every door, every fence, must be kept in repair."[24]

Booker responded to Ruffner's pushing him to excel. Years later, when he visited the Vermont home of Ruffner's birth, Washington removed his hat and bowed. "For me it is a shrine,"[25] he explained when someone asked him why.

Frederick Douglass

For decades, Frederick Douglass occupied the prominent position among African American leaders that Booker T. Washington eventually held. Born in slavery in Maryland in 1818, Douglass learned to read and write from the white children with whom he associated. He read as often as he could and encouraged other slaves to become literate. For those activities, a cruel slave master whipped Douglass repeatedly.

Douglass tried unsuccessfully to escape from his master twice. Finally, a third try in 1838 succeeded. He joined antislavery organizations in the North and often spoke to gatherings about his experiences as a slave. In 1845 he wrote his autobiography, the influential *Narrative of the Life of Frederick Douglass, an American Slave*, which became a best seller. In the

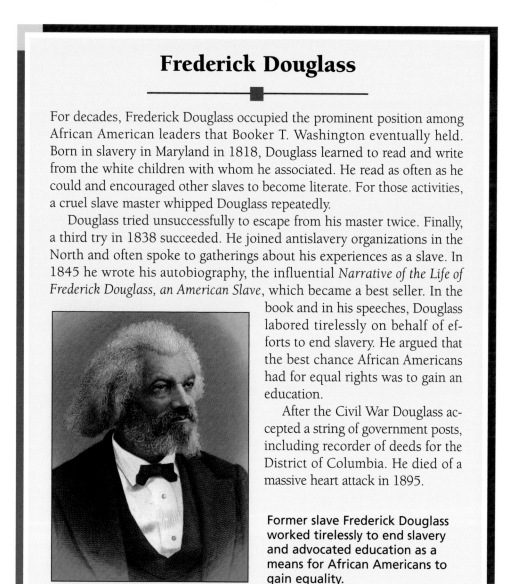

book and in his speeches, Douglass labored tirelessly on behalf of efforts to end slavery. He argued that the best chance African Americans had for equal rights was to gain an education.

After the Civil War Douglass accepted a string of government posts, including recorder of deeds for the District of Columbia. He died of a massive heart attack in 1895.

Former slave Frederick Douglass worked tirelessly to end slavery and advocated education as a means for African Americans to gain equality.

Booker also saw that Ruffner, born into poverty in Vermont, had succeeded due to hard work and determination. He concluded that if a white female could succeed, so could he. It affirmed his belief that "merit, no matter under what skin found, is, in the long run, recognized and rewarded." Washington adds that "the lessons that I learned in the home of Mrs. Ruffner were as valuable to me as any education I have ever gotten anywhere since."[26] What mattered to him most was that the lessons were practical and usable. It seemed to Booker that if a person followed the lessons, success would be achieved.

On most mornings, Ruffner allowed Booker to gather fruit and vegetables from the family garden and sell them door-to-door throughout the area. Ruffner trusted that Booker would hand to her every penny he collected, and her pupil never disappointed her. One day as Booker sold his fruit, an acquaintance walked up and took a peach without paying. Booker stopped the individual and explained if the fruit were his, he would willingly let him have it, but as Mrs. Ruffner had given the fruit to him and trusted him to properly handle it, he could not permit him to keep it without paying. The man argued that nobody would miss a single peach, but Booker remained adamant and retrieved the fruit.

Ruffner also encouraged Booker to read during his free moments. She sent him to William Davis's school whenever possible and helped him acquire a few secondhand books as the start of his first library. Booker often sat up at night reading while the rest of the household slept.

The gruff Ruffner took to Booker as if he were her son. She admired his determination and thoroughness and knew he could succeed. "His conduct has always been without fault, and what more can you wish?" she insisted. "He seemed peculiarly determined to emerge from his obscurity. He was ever restless, uneasy, as if knowing that contentment would mean inaction. 'Am I getting on?'—that was his principal question."[27]

To Hampton

Booker's next turn in life happened in almost an offhanded manner. While working at the mine he overheard two workers talking about a Virginia college that educated black students. Booker

Students attend class at Virginia's Hampton Institute. Upon hearing that a college for black students existed, Washington vowed to pursue his education there.

could hardly believe that such a place existed for former slaves in the South, but he decided to find out what he could about the institution.

The prospect of gaining a higher education excited Booker. "As they went on describing the school," Washington later recalled,

> it seemed to me that it must be the greatest place on earth, and not even Heaven presented more attractions for me at that time than did the Hampton Normal and Agricultural Institute in Virginia, about which these men were talking. I resolved at once to go to that school, although I had no idea where it was, or how many miles away, or how I was going to reach it; I remembered only that I was on fire constantly with one ambition, and that was to go to Hampton. This thought was with me day and night.[28]

Though Booker's mother worried that he pursued an unobtainable goal, other Malden blacks came to his assistance. His brother John saved whatever money he could from his jobs to raise funds for the trip to Hampton, as did older blacks who had spent a lifetime in slavery, thrilled with the chance of seeing one of their own heading off to a place like Hampton. They handed Booker pennies and nickels—a fortune to those scratching a meager life from the coal and salt mines—so that he might be able to leave.

Finally, in 1872 Booker accumulated enough money to start the four-hundred-mile trip to the school. He packed his few belongings in a solitary satchel, kissed his mother good-bye, and hopped first on a railroad, then a stagecoach.

Booker experienced the restrictions of southern society when the stagecoach stopped one night at a hotel. The customers, all white except for Booker, piled into the lobby seeking rooms, but the owner refused to admit a black person into his establishment. Booker had to sleep outside while the whites enjoyed a comfortable night inside. Washington later stated that this was the first time he experienced what being black in a society dominated by whites actually meant.

By the time the stagecoach reached Richmond, Virginia, Booker had run out of money. He had nothing to purchase the apple pies and fried chicken that vendors sold along the streets, and he slept that night underneath one of the city's wooden sidewalks. He used his satchel as a pillow and lay most of the time listening to walkers pass above him.

Fortunately, the captain of a ship docked in Richmond let Booker unload cargo from the vessel in exchange for food and money. Booker worked for the man until he had enough money to reach Hampton.

With fifty cents in his pocket, Booker started the final leg of his voyage to Hampton. The experience at Hampton would introduce Booker to a major role model and forge the philosophy that would guide his life.

Chapter Three

"I Had Reached the Promised Land"

Hampton Normal and Agricultural Institute was one of a handful of schools established in the South after the Civil War to educate black students. General Samuel C. Armstrong, a white former Union army officer, started Hampton in 1868. He focused on character and practical skills, such as crafts, home-making, and agriculture, that blacks could take with them after graduation to be self-sustaining individuals. He hoped that his students would then become role models for other blacks, "to train selected youth who shall go out and teach and lead their people,"[29] as he put it in advertising the school.

Armstrong urged his students to be thrifty and hardworking. He told them they could gain the community's respect by owning their own land. He believed that society would be changed the most through the example and labor of individuals doing what they could to improve their lot.

When Booker arrived in Hampton in 1872, he was about to meet the single most influential person in his life. Armstrong set an example that Booker Washington was to follow till death.

"A New Kind of Existence"

The initial sight of the Hampton Institute, which then consisted of a single three-story building, moved Booker to tears.

Virginia's Hampton Institute sits on the shore of Chesapeake Bay. Washington claimed to have been moved to tears the first time he saw the Hampton Institute.

After struggling his entire life, first in slavery and then in West Virginia's mines, he could barely contain his emotions as he stood along the road and gazed at the place that would give him an education. "It seemed to me to be the largest and most beautiful building I had ever seen," Washington writes in his autobiography. "The sight of it seemed to give me new life. I felt that a new kind of existence had now begun—that life would now have a new meaning. I felt that I had reached the promised land, and I resolved to let no obstacle prevent me from putting forth the highest effort to fit myself to accomplish the most good in the world."[30]

He walked up to the building hesitantly, but hopefully. Weary and dirty from the arduous trip, he walked inside for an interview with the assistant principal, Mary Mackie. Taken aback by his appearance, Mackie almost dismissed Booker on the spot, but the young man pled his case. She gave him an assignment as a sort of test—clean the adjoining room from top to bottom. Having been trained by the meticulous Ruffner, Booker knew he could handle the task with ease. When Mackie inspected the room—Washington swept the room three times and dusted it four times—she muttered, "I guess you will do to enter this institution"[31] and accepted him into Hampton.

To help cover his tuition, Mackie offered Booker a job as janitor. Though it meant he would have to rise at 4:00 each morning to start fires and labor far into the night cleaning rooms, he gladly accepted.

Booker, whom a classmate later described as "an innocent, green looking rustic West Virginia boy,"[32] had made it through the door, but entrance to Hampton demanded adjustments. Teachers handed him secondhand clothing to supplement the single change he brought with him, and he had to unobtrusively observe his fellow students to figure out what to do with bed sheets. That first night, having never slept in a freshly made bed, he had no idea what sheets were for and climbed in under both. The second night he lay on top of both sets, but then noticed how the other students in the dormitory room slid in between the top and bottom sheets.

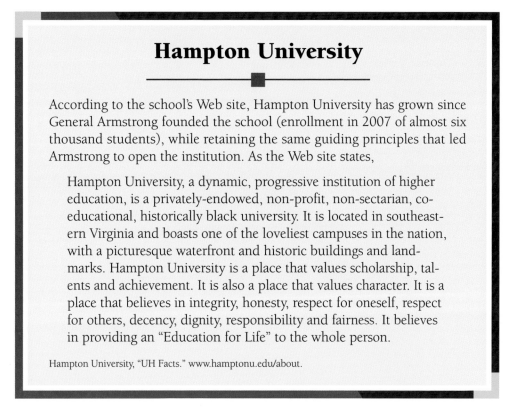

Hampton University

According to the school's Web site, Hampton University has grown since General Armstrong founded the school (enrollment in 2007 of almost six thousand students), while retaining the same guiding principles that led Armstrong to open the institution. As the Web site states,

> Hampton University, a dynamic, progressive institution of higher education, is a privately-endowed, non-profit, non-sectarian, co-educational, historically black university. It is located in southeastern Virginia and boasts one of the loveliest campuses in the nation, with a picturesque waterfront and historic buildings and landmarks. Hampton University is a place that values scholarship, talents and achievement. It is also a place that values character. It is a place that believes in integrity, honesty, respect for oneself, respect for others, decency, dignity, responsibility and fairness. It believes in providing an "Education for Life" to the whole person.

Hampton University, "UH Facts." www.hamptonu.edu/about.

A series of new situations gave Booker plenty to absorb. He had never eaten at regular hours, never used a napkin, never taken regular baths, and never used a toothbrush. They now became part of his daily regimen. It was a strange new world, but Booker was happy to learn its ways.

"The Noblest, Rarest Human Being"

Hampton altered Booker by bringing him into contact with Armstrong, who would mold Booker into the person he became. As soon as he met Armstrong, Booker felt he stood in the presence of greatness, calling him "the noblest, rarest human being that it has ever been my privilege to meet." Later in life, after he had met kings and presidents, famed authors and politicians, Washington

Former Union general Samuel Chapman Armstrong started the Hampton Institute in 1868 with the purpose of teaching character and practical skills to former slaves.

General Armstrong

■

Born on January 30, 1839, in Hawaii, Samuel Chapman Armstrong was the sixth of ten children. In 1860, one year before the Civil War started, he traveled to the mainland to study at Williams College in Massachusetts. Upon graduation, he joined the Union army as a captain in the 125th New York Volunteers, but he made his mark as a capable commander of African American soldiers, particularly the 9th Colored Troops.

When the war ended in 1865, Chapman turned to the education field. He started Hampton Institute in 1868 with fifteen students and one teacher but quickly expanded operations. Among his notable accomplishments, in addition to helping mold Washington and other African Americans, was his program to assist Native Americans, the first of whom arrived on campus in 1878.

General Armstrong died in 1893 at the age of fifty-four.

added, "It has been my fortune to meet personally many of what are called great characters, both in Europe and America, but I do not hesitate to say that I never met any man who, in my estimation, was the equal of General Armstrong."[33]

Armstrong demanded much from his students that had not been required of them, or even possible, in their lives as slaves. He conducted daily inspections of their beds and clothes and noted anything out of place. He expected cleanliness, including daily baths and cleaning of their teeth. Armstrong emphasized that through hard work, anyone could overcome obstacles. Booker and Armstrong became inseparable, with the student following the headmaster's advice and seeking his counsel. Armstrong became the father figure Booker never had.

That first year, Booker studied arithmetic, grammar, spelling, geography, natural history, and farm animals. He started to read the Bible daily and practiced the fundamentals of public speaking and debating. He impressed teachers with his diligence and desire to improve in any way possible.

What most impressed Booker was the willingness of his teachers to unselfishly assist their students. "It was hard for me to understand how any individuals could bring themselves to the point where they could be so happy in working for others. Before the end of the year I think I began learning that those that are happiest are those who do most for others."[34] It was another example that shaped Washington's character.

Selflessness abounded on the campus. That winter the dormitory lacked enough beds to house every student in the growing institution, so Armstrong asked for volunteers to sleep in tents. He did not have to ask a second time. "I was one of the volunteers," writes Washington. "The winter that we spent in those tents was an intensely cold one, and we suffered severely—how much I am sure General Armstrong never knew, because we made no complaints. It was enough for us to know that we were pleasing General Armstrong, and that we were making it possible for an additional number of students to secure an education."[35]

Return to Malden

Using money sent from his brother and some borrowed from a teacher, Booker was able to return to Malden after his second year at Hampton. The town welcomed him as a hero. Town residents flooded him with questions about his experiences, and invitations to dinner poured in. Booker spoke to Sunday church gatherings and to Sunday schools. He served as a role model to blacks in Malden, who saw that one could succeed with determination and persistence.

Jubilation came with sorrow, however, when Booker's mother, who had been a rock of stability for the family, passed away from ailments that dated back to the slave days. Booker and his family missed her strong hand and guidance in family matters. Ruffner eased some of their troubles with donations of money and food. The money enabled Booker to return to Hampton for his third and final year.

Graduation from Hampton

A goal drove Booker to work even harder his final year at Hampton —he hoped to be selected to deliver one of the speeches during the graduation ceremonies. After compiling an impressive record in world history, government, agriculture, and homemaking, Booker attained his objective.

During the graduation ceremony, Armstrong handed him a certificate stating that Booker T. Washington was competent to teach, which a proud Washington held as if it were a treasure. Another student observed Washington that day and later said that he looked "like a conqueror who had won a great victory."[36] In many ways he had, for he had overcome slavery and poverty to achieve this moment.

After graduating, Washington worked for a few months as a waiter at a luxury resort in Connecticut, then returned to Malden where he taught in a school for blacks. Washington relished the opportunity to help other people and even started a night school for the many blacks who worked during the day. He called this time in Malden one of the happiest experiences of his life.

Washington Mentors His Own Students

Washington followed the example of Armstrong, his mentor. He worked from early in the morning until late at night and insisted on cleanliness for each student. He preached that instead of relying on the government to improve their lives, as many former slaves were doing, they should look inward. He told his students that success came from hard work and overcoming obstacles. "I have begun everything with the idea that I could succeed, and I never had much patience with the multitudes of people who are always ready to explain why one cannot succeed."[37]

Washington also tried to impart useful information to his students. One day Washington struggled to keep the class's attention during a session on landforms. The series of questions he fired at the youths produced little more than perfunctory replies. During recess, Washington watched his students rush into the marshes to cool off by wading in the water. One student started pointing out tiny islands, peninsulas, and other miniature land forms in the marsh, which led to a barrage of shouts proclaiming the discovery of yet more. Washington concluded that his lesson had failed to show the relevance of the material to the students' lives, and vowed to make sure that did not happen again.

Washington produced such stellar students that Armstrong and others at Hampton labeled his graduates "Booker Washington's boys." They knew that any individual who came to them from the Malden school would be prepared, dedicated, and ready to work. Two of the students that Washington helped enter Hampton were his brother John and adopted brother James.

Washington's main value at Malden may have been similar to Armstrong's—he served as a powerful role model for others. One of his students said, "When I recall those early school days, I think of how proud we boys were to have one of us, who had been to college, come back and teach us. How our hearts swelled with the feeling that some day we would do likewise, and we went about our tasks with greater energy."[38]

In 1878, after three years teaching at Malden, Washington headed to Wayland Seminary in Washington, D.C., for a year of graduate training. Unlike Hampton, Wayland focused on academic instruction. Latin and Greek took the place of agriculture and crafts, and Washington felt the students at Wayland emerged far less ready to tackle larger issues than did the students at Hampton. They may have known how to read Latin texts, but Washington believed skills such as woodwork or farming would

Advice from Armstrong

——————■——————

Washington admired General Armstrong more than anyone he had met in life. He followed the man's example and advice and based his programs at Tuskegee after what he had observed at Hampton. A superb example of what attracted Washington are General Armstrong's words in an 1877 issue of Hampton's magazine, the *Southern Workman*.

Be thrifty and industrious. Command the respect of your neighbors by a good record and a good character. Own your own houses. Educate your children. Make the best of your difficulties. Live down prejudice. Cultivate peaceful relations with all. As a voter act as you think and not as you are told. Remember that you have seen marvellous changes in sixteen years [since the start of the Civil War]. In view of that be patient—thank God and take courage.

Quoted in Louis R. Harlan, *Booker T. Washington: The Making of a Black Leader, 1856–1901*. New York: Oxford University Press, 1972, p. 74.

help blacks advance. He also observed that many of his classmates had their tuition paid for them by parents, whereas students at Hampton worked to help pay for their education. He believed this made Wayland graduates less self-reliant.

"They seemed to give more attention to outward appearances," Washington concluded of his fashionably attired classmates. "In a word, they did not appear to me to be beginning at the bottom, on a real, solid foundation, to the extent that they were at Hampton. They knew more about Latin and Greek when they left school, but they seemed to know less about life and its conditions as they would meet it at their homes."[39]

Following his year at Wayland, Washington accepted an offer from a citizen's group in Charleston, West Virginia, to travel the state on the city's behalf in its campaign to be the new state capital. Charleston, which was only five miles from Malden, vied with two other cities for the honor. The winner would be decided in a statewide election, and the city leaders believed that Washington could swing many black votes its way. For three months Washington visited churches and assemblies, promoting the advantages of Charleston as the state capital. The experience provided Washington with valuable practice in the skill of public speaking and gained him acclaim when the state's residents selected Charleston as their choice.

"A Future Look in Your Eyes"

While Washington was involved in the state capital debate, he received an invitation from Armstrong to deliver the next graduation commencement address. He readily accepted, then prepared a speech he titled "The Force That Wins," a talk that emphasized the value of patience and hard work.

He must have impressed Armstrong and others at Hampton, for within a few weeks he received a second invitation—this one to teach at the institution for twenty-five dollars a month. Armstrong needed someone to supervise a new department for Native American youths and felt that Washington would be the ideal person.

Washington returned to Hampton in the fall of 1879. The school now boasted three hundred students, a staff of twenty-four, and featured departments in shoemaking, painting, carpentry, and blacksmithing. Washington moved into the dormitory set aside

The Hampton Institute quickly grew to include Native American students, who were initially supervised by Washington. They attended courses with African American students on practical skills such as carpentry.

for the Native Americans—called the Wigwam by fellow students —to serve as housefather and counselor for the seventy-five pupils. Washington forged a tight bond with his new students, who eagerly listened to his advice and followed his example. Washington's work at Hampton proved so successful that the next year the government established a second school for Native American youths at Carlisle Barracks, Pennsylvania.

Washington again faced the humiliating effects of segregation while traveling to Washington, D.C., with one of his Native American students. While aboard a steamboat, Washington and his student waited outside the dining room until all the white patrons had eaten, then headed inside. A worker halted the pair and informed Washington that while the Native American could sit at a table and enjoy a meal in the segregated quarters, Washington could not. Later during the trip, the pair walked into a Washington, D.C., hotel seeking rooms, but faced the same awkward situation. The student received a room while his teacher had to seek other accommodations, all on account of his skin color.

In addition to his Native American charges, Washington also supervised a night school. Some students had no money to pay tuition, so the school arranged for them to work in the school's carpentry shop or metal shop for ten hours each day, then attend school with Washington in the evening. Despite the rigorous schedule, Washington found that the individuals in what he called his "Plucky Class" worked harder than those he instructed during the day. "In all my teaching I never taught pupils who gave me such genuine satisfaction as these did,"[40] he boasted of the night students.

As proud as he was of his endeavors at Hampton, Washington believed that something greater lay ahead. Hampton was Armstrong's institution, not his, and Washington wanted to make his own mark. A student named W.T. McKinney said to Washington years later, "You always appeared to be looking for something in the distant future. There was always seen a future look in your eyes."[41]

The man and his mission were about to meet.

Chapter Four

"Making Bricks Without Straw"

Two Tuskegee, Alabama, citizens—Colonel C.F. Foster, a white Civil War veteran and former slave owner, and Tuskegee's leading black citizen, Lewis Adams—joined efforts to start a school for black students. They at first asked a white teacher to head the institution, but when he visited the town and discovered that practically nothing—no buildings, no staff—existed, he declined the offer. Whomever Foster and Adams selected would have to build the school from scratch.

In desperation, they asked Armstrong to recommend a white teacher. He wrote back that none came to mind, but that a promising black graduate might be what they were looking for. He described Washington's qualifications in such glowing terms that Foster and Adams quickly accepted. "Booker T. Washington will suit us," they wrote back. "Send him at once."[42] Once again the influence of Armstrong impacted Washington's life.

The Work Seemed Beyond Accomplishing

By the time Washington arrived in June 1881, the school's site featured two dilapidated structures—an old church and a run-down shanty—and a blind horse. Washington had to assemble a faculty, find students for them to teach, and somehow keep everyone happy until improved accommodations could be arranged. "The task before me did not seem a very encouraging one," he writes. "It seemed much like making bricks without straw."[43]

Washington immediately headed out to visit families in the Tuskegee area, believing that few students would enroll on their own account. He studied their lifestyles and habits while spreading the news of the new school and saw how economically depressed the inhabitants were. Struggling in the sharecropping system, where black farmers scratched out a meager existence farming white-owned land, the blacks worsened their plight by focusing solely on planting cotton to the exclusion of other crops that could be both sold and eaten, such as corn or beets. Black farmers and their families lived in squalid shacks and, because of horrible sanitary conditions, did not live as long as other Americans.

When Washington took over the Tuskegee Institute in 1881, the campus consisted of only a few basic buildings.

"I confess that what I saw during my month of travel and investigation left me with a very heavy heart. The work to be done in order to lift these people up seemed almost beyond accomplishing."[44] As depressing as the conditions were, Washington quickly saw the value of a school patterned after Hampton, where students learned skills they could use after graduation to better their lives.

While touring the area, Washington recruited students to his school. He asked young men and women what they sought for themselves and explained how the new school could help them realize their dreams. He also noticed how willing the young people were to gain a better life. They eagerly sought an education that might lift them out of the hopelessness that seemed to stifle their parents.

First Lessons at Tuskegee

On July 4, 1881, Washington opened Tuskegee Normal and Industrial Institute to its first thirty students, half male and half female. Though they ranged in age from the late teens to the mid-forties, Washington required that all be able to read and write. On the second day, Washington lined up his students for their first daily inspection, a rigorous examination of their clothing and cleanliness. He walked down the line pointing out broken or missing buttons, then ended by quizzing them on national and world events.

"He told us all about taking care of our bodies and ourselves," recalled one of the students years later. "Then we all had to wear neckties."[45] Washington felt that before an individual succeeded, he had to feel good about himself, and proper grooming was the first step.

Next came the educational aspect. Washington expected his students were used to memorizing facts and rules, a regimen that many schools emphasized. In Washington's opinion, this did little to prepare the charges for the world outside of school. He wanted graduates to return to their homes with skills to help both their communities and families.

Even Washington's curriculum grew out of necessity. "We began with agriculture because we had to eat,"[46] he later explained. By teaching agriculture, he was feeding the students as well as imparting a useful talent.

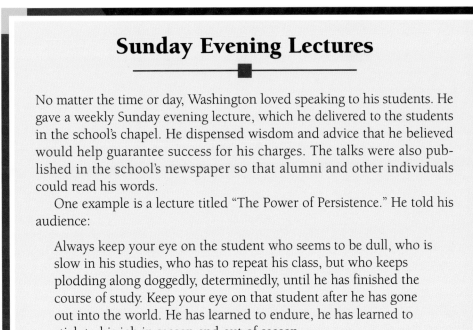

Sunday Evening Lectures

No matter the time or day, Washington loved speaking to his students. He gave a weekly Sunday evening lecture, which he delivered to the students in the school's chapel. He dispensed wisdom and advice that he believed would help guarantee success for his charges. The talks were also published in the school's newspaper so that alumni and other individuals could read his words.

One example is a lecture titled "The Power of Persistence." He told his audience:

Always keep your eye on the student who seems to be dull, who is slow in his studies, who has to repeat his class, but who keeps plodding along doggedly, determinedly, until he has finished the course of study. Keep your eye on that student after he has gone out into the world. He has learned to endure, he has learned to stick to his job in season and out of season.

Quoted in Emmett J. Scott and Lyman Beecher Stowe, *Booker T. Washington: Builder of a Civilization.* Garden City, NY: Doubleday, Page, 1918, p. 235.

Washington faced initial resistance from some of the students, who argued that rather than working the fields, they should receive an education that focused on the classics of literature, philosophy, and other similar subjects. Washington answered by grabbing some tools and heading to the farmland.

When I explained my plan to the young men, I noticed that they did not seem to take to it very kindly. It was hard for them to see the connection between clearing land and an education. Besides, many of them had been school-teachers, and they questioned whether or not clearing land would be in keeping with their dignity. In order to relieve them from any embarrassment, each afternoon after school I took my axe and led the way to the woods. When they saw that I was not afraid or ashamed to work, they began to assist with more enthusiasm. We kept at the work each afternoon,

The curriculum at Tuskegee emphasized agriculture skills, not only because they would be useful to the students outside of school, but also because farming activities allowed the school to grow much of its own food.

until we had cleared about twenty acres and had planted a crop.[47]

A few students dropped out, but Washington pursued what he believed was the best path toward a decent living for his charges. Despite the resistance and a few dropouts, by the end of the first month word had spread of Washington's school to such an extent that the student body nearly doubled in size.

By summer's end Washington located an abandoned plantation that had a small cabin, a stable, a chicken house, and a kitchen. Washington lacked the five hundred dollars needed to purchase the place. As he often did in those early years, he turned to Hampton for assistance, where he received a loan to cover the costs.

Fund-Raising Difficulties

To meet the demands of the growing school population, Washington hired Olivia A. Davidson as a teacher. She arrived in August, less than two months after Washington first opened the doors, and soon became one of the headmaster's most trusted employees.

Davidson used connections with wealthy industrialists and supporters living in the East to raise much-needed funds for Tuskegee, while Washington relied on letters of introduction from Armstrong to convince people to contribute. Most weekends, one or both were absent from Tuskegee, seeking to bring in dollars to pay the rapidly growing mound of bills. Davidson organized charity bazaars, and both traveled door-to-door in search of more money. Poor black farmers in the region sensed that Washington was accomplishing something to help African Americans and

Washington worked hard to raise funds for Tuskegee. He eventually found charitable institutions willing to help.

contributed pennies and nickels. One elderly woman, a former slave, told Washington she had no money to help out, but hoped that the six eggs she donated would somehow aid the students in achieving their education.

"During the first years at Tuskegee I recall that night after night I would roll and toss on my bed, without sleep, because of the anxiety and uncertainty which we were in regarding money." Washington understood the importance of keeping the school in operation for a group of people trying to escape the clutches of slavery. "I knew that if we failed it would injure the whole race. I knew that the presumption was against us. I knew that in the case of white people beginning such an enterprise it would be taken for granted that they were going to succeed, but in our case I felt that people would be surprised if we succeeded."[48]

He gradually found charitable institutions willing to help. In 1883 the Slater and the Peabody funds granted Washington the money to build a carpenter shop and a windmill and to purchase a sewing machine, mules, and a wagon—all items that helped further his approach of teaching practical skills.

Practical Lessons

Washington utilized the lessons he learned from Ruffner and Armstrong.

Besides the insistence on cleanliness, no student arriving late for dinner would be fed, alcohol and tobacco were banned, and playing cards or dice could get a student expelled.

Washington stipulated a purpose for each hour of the day, which began at 5:00 A.M. and ended with lights out at 9:30 P.M. Classroom sessions filled the mornings. While the students learned mathematics and language, the subjects were connected as much as possible to problems or issues they would face in society. For instance, the spelling words might be a list of farm implement names or machinery parts, while the math teacher might assign a problem dealing with how many bales of cotton could be stored in a room of a certain size. In the afternoon, students headed to the barn and fields to complete chores or till the land.

Washington even used Sundays to convey his message. He spoke to evening student assemblies about topics such as, "Helping Others," "Have You Done Your Best?" and "A Penny Saved."

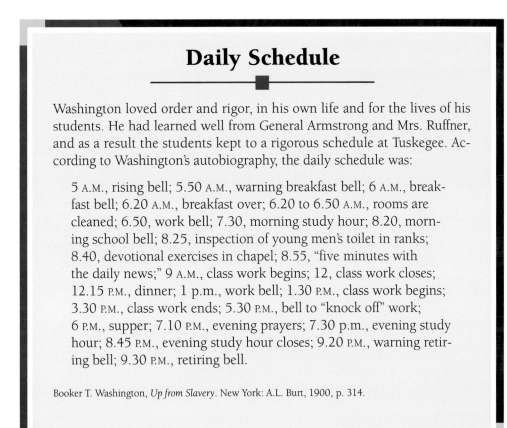

Daily Schedule

Washington loved order and rigor, in his own life and for the lives of his students. He had learned well from General Armstrong and Mrs. Ruffner, and as a result the students kept to a rigorous schedule at Tuskegee. According to Washington's autobiography, the daily schedule was:

> 5 A.M., rising bell; 5.50 A.M., warning breakfast bell; 6 A.M., breakfast bell; 6.20 A.M., breakfast over; 6.20 to 6.50 A.M., rooms are cleaned; 6.50, work bell; 7.30, morning study hour; 8.20, morning school bell; 8.25, inspection of young men's toilet in ranks; 8.40, devotional exercises in chapel; 8.55, "five minutes with the daily news;" 9 A.M., class work begins; 12, class work closes; 12.15 P.M., dinner; 1 p.m., work bell; 1.30 P.M., class work begins; 3.30 P.M., class work ends; 5.30 P.M., bell to "knock off" work; 6 P.M., supper; 7.10 P.M., evening prayers; 7.30 p.m., evening study hour; 8.45 P.M., evening study hour closes; 9.20 P.M., warning retiring bell; 9.30 P.M., retiring bell.

Booker T. Washington, *Up from Slavery*. New York: A.L. Burt, 1900, p. 314.

He did not want to waste a moment in helping prepare his students for the challenges he knew awaited them once they left Tuskegee.

Tuskegee Expands

Washington expanded Tuskegee when need demanded it and when money allowed it. He started a brick-making enterprise in 1883 so he could more cheaply construct new buildings on the grounds. The Tuskegee area contained clay soil that was excellent for making bricks, so Washington decided to combine the benefits of possessing his own brick-making enterprise—a boon to his school—while at the same time introducing his students to a new trade. He also contended that once Tuskegee produced bricks that Tuskegee and surrounding communities could use, the local inhabitants would see the school's value and better support its labors. Some of the students detested the work, which required them to jump into a mud pit, but to calm their doubts Washington jumped in with them. That same year he added a carpentry department, and two years later he started a printing department so that he could better advertise his school. A monthly newsletter, *Southern Letter*, was the result.

The school expanded in other ways. In 1883 he dedicated Porter Hall, a three-story building housing classrooms, a chapel, and a girls' dormitory, in honor of A.H. Porter of New York, whose five-hundred-dollar donation was then the largest to date. In 1884

Tuskegee students stack bricks as part of the school's foray into the trade, which was both a means of providing materials for buildings on campus and a money-making enterprise.

he started a night school for those who lacked money yet sought an education. Imitating Armstrong's work at the Hampton Institute, Washington required the night school students to work in one of Tuskegee's departments for ten hours a day, which earned tuition money, then attend class at night for two hours.

In 1887 Washington added cabinet- and mattress-making departments, one year before wheel making and wagon building joined the curriculum. In 1889 students could take classes in shoe making, harness making, and metal work.

To mark the school's growth and to celebrate its success, in 1888 Washington held an anniversary ceremony. Two thousand people, including black and white citizens from Tuskegee and nearby towns, listened to speeches and examined work completed by student farmers or carpenters and marveled at the four major buildings that now stood upon the grounds, including Alabama Hall and Armstrong Hall.

A Practical Approach to Gaining Equality

By now word had spread of Washington's school and of his views on how blacks could attain a better life in a white-dominated society. He argued that although blacks were now free, true equality would arrive in stages rather than all at once. Before reaching that elusive goal, the former slaves would have to prove their worth, which Washington contended could best be accomplished by learning the skills that society most needed. "We had scores of young men learned in Greek, but few in carpentry or mechanical drawing. We had trained many in Latin, but almost none as engineers, bridge-builders, and machinists. Numbers were taken from the farm and educated, but were educated in everything else except agriculture."[49]

Washington argued for practicality. Instead of planting cotton on every plot of land, which most black farmers tended to do in the Civil War's aftermath, he urged that they plant crops that could be eaten by the farmer and his family in addition to being sold, which could not be done with cotton. It made more sense to Washington to eat what is needed and sell the remainder in town.

Washington thought that if blacks would show southern society that they possessed valuable skills and could produce what the community needed, then they could move toward complete

Students at the Tuskegee Institute spent much of their time in workshops learning practical skills, which Washington felt was a key factor in the achievement of economic equality once they were out of school.

equality—the social and political realms. Washington believed that whites would be more willing to work with blacks in the economic arena first, then grudgingly draw closer together in the social realm. Thus he emphasized brick making, carpentry, and farming skills over academic knowledge and aggressive campaigns to enjoy full equality. "I tried to emphasize the fact that while the Negro should not be deprived by unfair means of the franchise [voting], political agitation alone would not save him, and that back of the ballot he must have property, industry, skill, economy, intelligence, and character, and that no race without these elements could permanently succeed."[50]

"A World of Unpleasant Facts"

Washington did not abandon the drive to full equality; he believed that in the white-dominated southern society blacks had to progress slowly. Blacks could not push whites away with extreme demands for complete equality right away—they had to first prove their worth and gain a solid economic foundation.

Some critics believed that Washington abandoned full equality for economic success, but others argued that all Washington did was work within the white-dominated system in which he lived.

Washington promoted these views as the best way to overcome the disadvantages blacks faced in a society that handed more rights to whites. In the aftermath of the Civil War, state legislatures in the South passed laws restricting the rights of the former slaves. Laws banned interracial marriages and required separate accommodations for blacks and whites on railroads and in hotels, barbershops, schools, and restaurants. Many whites even feared that educating the former slaves would stir agitation. "This education is ruining our Negroes," stated Mississippi politician J.K. Vardman. "They're demanding equality."[51]

Some southern whites preferred Washington's views on black education because they incorrectly assumed the black educator had given up on complete equality and focused instead on professions that many whites did not care to enter. According to President Theodore Roosevelt, that was not true. "He kept his

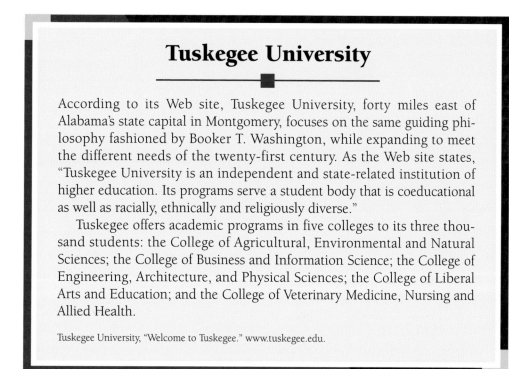

Tuskegee University

According to its Web site, Tuskegee University, forty miles east of Alabama's state capital in Montgomery, focuses on the same guiding philosophy fashioned by Booker T. Washington, while expanding to meet the different needs of the twenty-first century. As the Web site states, "Tuskegee University is an independent and state-related institution of higher education. Its programs serve a student body that is coeducational as well as racially, ethnically and religiously diverse."

Tuskegee offers academic programs in five colleges to its three thousand students: the College of Agricultural, Environmental and Natural Sciences; the College of Business and Information Science; the College of Engineering, Architecture, and Physical Sciences; the College of Liberal Arts and Education; and the College of Veterinary Medicine, Nursing and Allied Health.

Tuskegee University, "Welcome to Tuskegee." www.tuskegee.edu.

high ideals, always; but he never forgot for a moment that he was living in an actual world of three dimensions, in a world of unpleasant facts, where those unpleasant facts had to be faced; and he made the best possible out of a bad situation from which there was no ideal best to be obtained."[52] Washington was a practical man who worked in the here and now to improve life for blacks, not an idealist who pushed for gains that might not arrive for a generation or more.

Family Life and Public Speaking

In the midst of building Tuskegee, Washington found time to start a family. In 1882 he married Fanny N. Smith. The couple gave birth to daughter Portia in 1883, the first child born on the Tuskegee campus, but the next year Fanny suddenly died when she fell from a wagon. The loss devastated Washington, who found great comfort amid his hectic schedule with his wife and child.

Washington remarried in 1885, this time to his assistant at Tuskegee, Olivia A. Davidson. The two shared happy moments at home and had two sons, Booker Jr. and Ernest. At school they worked tirelessly to keep Tuskegee going. In addition to making numerous fund-raising trips, Davidson took the female students under her wing. She was like a second mother to many of the girls. The sadness Washington felt after Fanny's death dissipated during his time with Olivia. Then, tragically, Olivia died in 1889. Washington blamed himself for this loss, stating that Olivia succumbed from overwork. "She literally wore herself out in her never ceasing efforts in behalf of the work that she so dearly loved."[53] Within seven years Washington had married twice, saw the birth of three children, and buried two wives.

He sought solace in his work, which by the mid-1880s was beginning to attract attention all around the United States. In the summer of 1884 he received an invitation to address a meeting of the National Education Association in Madison, Wisconsin. It would be the first talk he would deliver to a large national audience. Washington understood the impact this speech could have, so he carefully prepared what he would say. In his speech Washington urged blacks to purchase their own land, even if they had to start with a single acre, and stated that if they showed a willingness to work hard and produce items of value, they would

The home at which Washington and his family lived on the Tuskegee campus was known as The Oaks.

enjoy the cooperation of white southerners. The way to progress was to start at the bottom and work your way upward. "In a rich and prosperous country like America," he told the crowd, "there is absolutely no excuse for persons living in idleness. I have little patience with persons who go round whining that they cannot find anything to do."[54]

This speech was important in that it gave Washington national exposure. More invitations to speak at prominent gatherings came in, and additional attention came both to Tuskegee and to Washington's views.

The educator was about to step onto the national platform.

Chapter Five

"The Ascendancy of Mr. Booker T. Washington"

As Washington's fame spread, other organizations sought his help. In 1895 a group of Georgia citizens was petitioning Congress for financial assistance for their mammoth Cotton States and International Exhibition scheduled to be held in Atlanta. They asked Washington to speak on their behalf. His fifteen-minute delivery to Congress gained significant support for the exposition among the politicians.

An Important Invitation

Impressed with Washington's labors on their behalf, exposition officials invited the educator to speak during the exposition itself. They took a big step, as this was the first time that an African American had been asked to speak before an audience of so many whites, containing numerous influential business-people and financiers. Washington knew that his words could either help blacks move forward in the South or could raise animosity among whites and hinder the efforts of blacks. He decided to adopt a positive approach that emphasized what blacks had done without condemning white hostility toward African Americans.

The enormity of the task before him caused some acquaintances of Washington to doubt whether he should have taken on the challenge. A white Tuskegee resident said to him one day before he left for Atlanta, "Washington, you have spoken before the Northern white people, the Negroes in the South, and to us country white people in the South; but in Atlanta, tomorrow, you

Washington, shown here circa 1890, gained national prominence with his speech at the Cotton States and International Exhibition in 1895.

will have before you the Northern whites, the Southern whites, and the Negroes all together. I am afraid that you have got yourself into a tight place."[55]

Washington put more effort into preparing this speech than any other. He delivered the talk to his faculty and sought their comments, and he asked family and friends for their thoughts. He seemed to carry the burdens of an entire race of people, hardworking individuals he feared disappointing should he fail to properly move his audience.

"I prepared myself as best I could for the address, but as the eighteenth of September drew nearer, the heavier my heart became, and the more I feared that my effort would prove a failure and a disappointment." Washington slept little the night before, and the next morning "I went carefully over what I intended to say. I also kneeled down and asked God's blessing upon my effort."[56] Washington adds, "I felt a good deal as I suppose a man feels when he is on his way to the gallows."[57]

The Atlanta Speech

More than fifty thousand spectators packed the auditorium to hear the man from Tuskegee. Polite applause from a mixed crowd greeted his arrival, and attendees listened avidly as Washington repeated some of the thoughts he had expressed in earlier talks. He urged fellow blacks to focus on agriculture, crafts, and other professions that would bring them money. "No race can prosper till it learns that there is as much dignity in tilling a field as in writing a poem. It is at the bottom of life we must begin, and not at the top. Nor should we permit our grievances to overshadow our opportunities."[58] He told the black attendees, "The opportunity to earn a dollar in a factory just now is worth infinitely more than the opportunity to spend a dollar in an opera house."[59]

He then turned his comments toward the white southerners in the crowd and asked for their cooperation.

> Cast down your bucket among these people who have, without strikes and labour wars, tilled your fields, cleared your forests, builded your railroads and cities, and brought forth treasures from the bowels of the earth, and helped make possible this magnificent representation of the

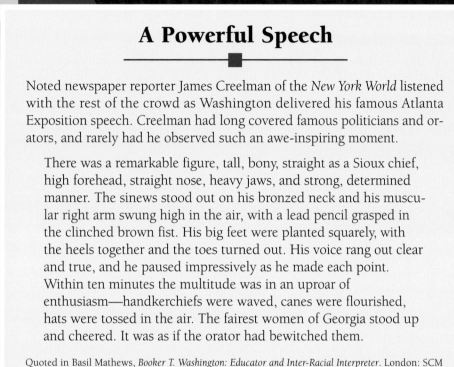

A Powerful Speech

Noted newspaper reporter James Creelman of the *New York World* listened with the rest of the crowd as Washington delivered his famous Atlanta Exposition speech. Creelman had long covered famous politicians and orators, and rarely had he observed such an awe-inspiring moment.

> There was a remarkable figure, tall, bony, straight as a Sioux chief, high forehead, straight nose, heavy jaws, and strong, determined manner. The sinews stood out on his bronzed neck and his muscular right arm swung high in the air, with a lead pencil grasped in the clinched brown fist. His big feet were planted squarely, with the heels together and the toes turned out. His voice rang out clear and true, and he paused impressively as he made each point. Within ten minutes the multitude was in an uproar of enthusiasm—handkerchiefs were waved, canes were flourished, hats were tossed in the air. The fairest women of Georgia stood up and cheered. It was as if the orator had bewitched them.

Quoted in Basil Mathews, *Booker T. Washington: Educator and Inter-Racial Interpreter*. London: SCM Press, 1949, p. 85.

progress of the South. Casting down your bucket among my people, helping and encouraging them as you are doing on these grounds, and to education of head, hand, and heart, you will find that they will buy your surplus land, make blossom the waste places in your fields, and run your factories.[60]

He warned that the black population in the South could be a cornerstone of a new South or could pose a large obstacle to progress, depending on how white southerners reacted.

Nearly sixteen millions of hands will aid you in pulling the load upward, or they will pull against you the load downward. We shall constitute one-third and more of the ignorance and crime of the South, or one-third its intelligence and progress; we shall contribute one-third to the business and industrial prosperity of the South, or we shall prove a veritable body of death, stagnating, depressing, retarding every effort to advance the body politic.[61]

Washington then headed into new territory and discussed the issue of social equality and race relations. He had always avoided this sensitive arena. He figured that in the volatile conditions that existed in the postwar South, he would achieve more by concentrating on the economic realm, but the time and the audience were right. He spoke the words that are considered some of the most important in American history. "In all things that are purely social we can be as separate as the fingers, yet one as the hand in all things essential to mutual progress."[62]

These closing words, spoken at a time when Washington and other black leaders believed that a cautious approach to race relations was necessary, were later seized upon by critics as proof that Washington had abandoned the quest for social equality. At the time, however, the words received a standing ovation in the auditorium and near-universal acclaim in the country's newspapers. Reporters wrote that people waved handkerchiefs and tossed their hats into the air in jubilation and that tears streamed down the faces of black spectators over Washington's words. Georgia's governor, a powerful white politician, ran across the stage to shake Washington's hand. The speech propelled the Tuskegee educator to national prominence.

A Solid Arrangement for Blacks and Whites

Adulation followed Washington after the speech. He had difficulty leaving the building to return to the railroad station, and jubilant crowds waited to greet him at each stop along the route. Reporters labeled him the "Negro Moses," and President Grover Cleveland sent a congratulatory letter praising the address.

Newspapers heaped more acclaim on Washington. The *Atlanta Constitution* stated that Washington established a foundation upon which people of both races could construct improved relations. The Boston *Transcript* claimed Washington's talk overshadowed every other event at the exposition. Black newspapers hailed the words, and W.E.B. Du Bois, another leading black educator, agreed that Washington had proposed a solid arrangement. "I regarded his Atlanta speech as a statesmanlike effort to reach understanding with the white South; I hoped the South would respond with equal generosity and thus the nation could come to understanding for both races."[63] He added later, "Easily the most striking thing in the history of the American Negro since 1876 is the ascendancy of Mr. Booker T. Washington."[64]

Invitations to speak poured into Tuskegee. Washington gave as many as eight speeches a day, always emphasizing the progress that American blacks had made since slavery and offering what he saw as a workable solution to the problems facing blacks. He tried to find a common ground for southern whites, northern whites, and blacks, and praised the progress that had been made rather than denouncing white bigotry. He repeated his view that one day blacks would enjoy complete equality, but that for the time being they had to focus on developing their

After his impressive appearance at the Cotton States and International Exhibition, Washington was in high demand as a public speaker, promoting his views on economic equality. Here he addresses a crowd in Mississippi.

W.E.B. Du Bois

W.E.B. Du Bois was born on February 23, 1868, in Great Barrington, Massachusetts. The taunts directed his way by white students caused Du Bois to labor on behalf of his race, and at age fifteen he became a correspondent for the *New York Globe*.

He received a scholarship to attend Fisk University in Tennessee, where he saw firsthand the effects of segregation. After graduation, he headed to Harvard University to obtain a degree in history, then traveled to Europe for further study.

He established his reputation as an astute observer of civil rights in 1896, when he examined the conditions of African Americans living in Philadelphia, Pennsylvania. His book *The Philadelphia Negro* was the first extensive study about African Americans in the nation. His widespread fame pitted him against Booker T. Washington, who until then was the unquestioned spokesman for African Americans.

Du Bois continued to pursue equal rights aggressively throughout his life. In the 1950s he attacked the U.S. government's foreign policy, which he concluded was designed to force other people to live under a white-dominated system of government like that of the United States. He lived most of his later years in Europe and Africa and died in Ghana on August 27, 1963.

economic foundation. Once that was established, work toward social and political equality could proceed.

Some people interpreted Washington's words to indicate that, in exchange for a degree of economic stability, he was willing to forsake demands for complete equality, say little about unjust laws, and even overlook the violence directed toward blacks. Washington never intended that, however. Washington always claimed that he was willing to defer the dream of equal rights, but he never abandoned it. He believed he and other black leaders had to work within the system that existed and as such had to make compromises.

Three years later he gave proof of that when speaking of the sacrifices made by black soldiers in the recent Spanish-American

War. He stated that men who fight and die for a country deserve to be treated with dignity and respect. "When you have gotten the full story or the heroic conduct of the Negro in the Spanish-American war, have heard it from the lips of Northern soldier and Southern soldier, from ex-abolitionist and ex-masters, then decide within yourselves whether a race that is thus willing to die for its country should not be given the highest opportunity to live for its country."[65]

"We Are Coming Up"

When Frederick Douglass, who had been the undisputed leader of African Americans since before the Civil War, died a few months

Washington, shown here speaking to a large crowd of dignitaries and a group of students, became a tireless spokesman on issues affecting African American citizens.

after Washington's Atlanta speech, most naturally looked to Washington to fill the void. For the next ten years he was recognized as the spokesman for his race. When a politician needed advice, they sought Washington. When a school for black students needed funds, a word of support from Washington brought in thousands of dollars. Black and white citizens fashioned their opinions on civil rights based on what the educator said.

Presidents consulted Washington when dealing with issues concerning black citizens or when considering an African American for a political office. The day he assumed the presidency after William McKinley's assassination, Theodore Roosevelt sent a letter to Washington asking his advice.

A symbol that he had been accepted into the upper stratum of society came in June 1896, when the nation's most prominent university, Harvard, gave Washington an honorary master of arts degree. The occasion, which marked the first time that Harvard had bestowed such an honor on an African American, deeply moved the educator.

Washington took the occasion of his acceptance speech at Harvard to remind the audience of what blacks had accomplished and what yet needed to be done. He proclaimed that

> by the way of the shop, the field, the skilled hand, the habits of thrift and economy, by way of industrial school and college, we are coming up. We are crawling up, working up, yea, bursting up. Often through oppression, unjust discrimination and prejudice, but through them all, we are coming up; and with proper habits, intelligence and property, there is no power on earth that can permanently stay our progress.[66]

After outlining the steps that had already been taken, Washington looked to the immediate future, which would prove decisive to blacks around the country.

> During the next half-century and more, my race must continue passing through the severe American crucible. We are to be tested in our patience, our forbearance, our perseverance, our power to endure wrong, to withstand temptations, to economize, to acquire and use skill; in our ability

to compete, to succeed in commerce, to disregard the su-
perficial for the real, the appearance for the substance, to
be great and yet small, learned and yet simple, high and
yet the servant of all.[67]

"Make Your Own Little Heaven"

Washington's renown across the nation had benefits for Tuskegee.
Prominent scientists and professors joined the faculty, including
George Washington Carver, who arrived in 1896 to head the
school's agricultural program. Carver's research led to new farming methods that improved crop yields. For example, the bushels
of sweet potatoes per acre (0.4ha) increased from 37 bushels (1t)
to 266 bushels (7t), and the amount of cotton grown per acre
more than doubled. Tuskegee began publishing a calendar that
told farmers what to plant and when to plant it and pamphlets
instructing farmers on how to best utilize their land.

Washington arranged for wealthy northern business owners
to visit the Tuskegee campus so they could see for themselves the

Researcher and scientist George Washington Carver arrived at the
Tuskegee Institute in 1896 to lead the school's agriculture program,
one of many prominent educators to join the school's faculty.

Prominent politicians, businessmen, and philanthropists joined
Washington, third from front left, to celebrate Tuskegee's twenty-
fifth anniversary in April 1906, including (from left) politician and
journalist George McAneny, Hampton president Robert Ogden,
philanthropist J. G. Phelps Stokes, the Reverend Lyman Abbott, steel
baron Andrew Carnegie, H. B. Trissell, and Harvard president Charles
W. Eliot.

work that was being done at the institution. Once they observed
the students laboring at various crafts and heard Washington's
story of rising from slavery, they opened their wallets to offer donations. H.H. Rogers of Standard Oil, William H. Baldwin of
Southern Railway, and Andrew Carnegie of United States Steel
became major benefactors of Tuskegee. In 1898 President McKinley even stopped by for a visit. Washington's newfound status enabled him to arrange a permanent endowment for Tuskegee that
by the time of his death had accumulated $2 million, one of the
largest of all southern colleges.

In 1906 Washington arranged a splendid celebration to honor the school's twenty-fifth anniversary. Prominent individuals, such as future president William H. Taft, spoke and pointed to the 1,600 students, 83 buildings, and 156 faculty members as proof of Washington's success.

At the same time, Washington expanded the school's programs to benefit more people. A yearly Tuskegee Negro Conference brought black farmers and scientists together to discuss newer techniques and to share success stories. The popular events drew more than a thousand people, and Washington never failed to remind them that they had the power to "make your own little heaven right here and now."[68]

Tuskegee Outreach

For those who could not attend, Washington arranged for wagons to be sent to them. The wagons, driven by instructors, contained modern farm tools, chickens, corn, and oats. At each stop the instructor spoke about new methods, then headed to the field to plow a strip of land as a demonstration.

Washington's Farmers' Short Course, a two-week program studying advanced farming techniques, improved the economic lives of hundreds of farmers. Teachers displayed new and improved seeds, showed how to repair tools, how to plant and maintain small gardens, and how to rid their farms of pests.

Washington also started a night school for ministers, a building and loan association to assist people in obtaining homes, a library for the children of Tuskegee, a Negro county fair, and smaller schools in the countryside to educate poor blacks. Washington had one aim with all these programs—to improve the lives of poor farmers and start them on the path to a better life. His fame with these programs spread to such an extent that the governments of Great Britain, Germany, and Belgium asked Washington to send staff members to teach their farmers how to improve crop yields.

Washington did not confine his efforts to agriculture. He gathered a group of black teachers from different states to discuss common issues. From this gathering the National Association of Colored Teachers arose. In 1900 he helped organize the National Negro Business League so that successful black businessmen

Washington, third from left, poses with the executive committee of the National Negro Business League, which he helped organize in 1900.

could gather and share their ideas. This led to the creation of more groups, each focusing on a specific area. Organizations were formed for black lawyers, tailors, insurance agents, and newspaper reporters. The overriding idea was that if a person could produce a better product, customers would flock to the business no matter what color the owner was.

Personal Fame Grows

The publication of Washington's autobiography in 1900, *Up from Slavery*, gained worldwide attention for the educator and his labors. The best-selling book was translated into more languages than any other book from the United States at the time and brought more money to Tuskegee than all his other programs combined. People responded to the story of a man who rose from poverty to attain great heights.

The increased demands took a toll on Washington's health. Wealthy friends from Boston, Massachusetts, raised money to send Washington and his third wife (he had married Margaret

Murray, a Tuskegee teacher, in 1891) on an extended vacation to Europe. They collected enough donations to make up for the funds Washington would have raised by giving speeches around the nation during that time.

Within a day of leaving New York on May 10, 1899, Washington relaxed. "As soon as the last good-byes were said, and the steamer had cut loose from the wharf, the load of care, anxiety, and responsibility which I had carried for eighteen years began to lift itself from my shoulders at the rate, it seemed to me, of a pound a minute. It was the first time in all those years that I had felt, even in a measure, free from care."[69] He slept up to fifteen hours a day, and in one momentous afternoon he enjoyed tea with Queen Victoria of England.

A White House Dinner

Additional fame had other drawbacks. On October 16, 1901, Roosevelt invited Washington to dine with him at the White House, a move unheard of in the climate of the times. The two

President Theodore Roosevelt, right, is depicted hosting Washington at a White House dinner in October 1901.

White House Dinner

―――――■―――――

The furor aroused by Theodore Roosevelt's dinner invitation to Booker T. Washington produced hundreds of scathing remarks in the press, mainly in southern publications. However, a smattering of newspaper editorials, mainly from northern publications, endorsed the president's actions. The *New York World* believed the nation should be ashamed of a reaction that judges a man's dignity on the basis of skin color.

An American named Washington, one of the most learned, most eloquent, most brilliant men of the day, the President of a college, is asked to dinner by President Roosevelt. And because the pigment of his skin is some shades darker than that of others, a large part of the United States is convulsed with shame and rage.

Quoted in Mark Sullivan, *Our Times: The United States, 1900–1925*, vol. 3, *Pre-War America*. New York: Charles Scribner's Sons, 1930, p. 136.

enjoyed dinner with a few of Roosevelt's family members, then discussed southern politics and its relation to the race issue. A reporter for the Associated Press stopped at the White House to routinely scan the list of visitors that day, and matter-of-factly sent out the information that Washington had dined with the president.

The news spread about the nation like lightning. One black citizen telegraphed the White House that a white president inviting a black educator to the White House was the "greatest step for the race in a generation." Many white publications reacted venomously, however. One New Orleans, Louisiana, editor called Roosevelt the "worst enemy to his race of any white man who has ever occupied so high a place in the republic,"[70] and the *Memphis Scimitar* wrote, "The most damnable outrage which has ever been perpetrated by any citizen of the United States was committed yesterday by the President, when he invited a nigger to dine with him at the White House."[71]

Both Roosevelt and Washington received death threats in the dinner's aftermath, and police patrolled Tuskegee's campus in case an assassin appeared. Roosevelt was as stunned as Washington, but vowed not to be swayed by the bigoted reaction. "No one could possibly be as astonished as I was," he told a friend. Despite the bitter criticism, Roosevelt asserted, "I shall have him to dine as often as I please."[72]

Washington was learning that as his fame rose, criticism increased. At first it originated from white southerners. It soon would come from fellow black leaders.

Chapter Six

"To Make Carpenters Men"

As the twentieth century arrived, blacks still faced rigid discrimination. Despite the end of slavery and the efforts of men like Washington, many African Americans took a more aggressive approach to the race issue. Rather than quietly work toward a better economic life in the present as a foundation for equality later, as Washington urged, these new leaders demanded immediate equality. Washington became the object of caustic criticism.

Jim Crow

The new leaders had much ammunition. All they had to do was point to the numerous inequalities that still existed, especially in the South. Prospective black voters often had to pass a literacy test before being able to vote, whereas white voters did not. States banned interracial marriages, established separate school systems, and segregated railroad travel, buses, hospitals, and public washrooms.

Advocates of equality strongly urged Washington to condemn these and other practices of what was labeled the Jim Crow system, but Washington declined to speak out. He had worked for the past twenty years to create a workable system at

Tuskegee, and he feared that if he too strongly criticized the South he would endanger those gains. Like a protective father, he wanted to safeguard what he had nurtured. He also feared that if he became too militant he would frighten many of the donors whose dollars kept Tuskegee going. Thus he attempted to walk a fine line between acceptance and condemnation of discrimination, which made him an easy target from both sides.

Washington contended that if more individuals followed his path—gaining acceptance through economic success—they would enjoy greater rewards more quickly. "Whether in the North or South," he stated, "wherever I have seen a black man who was succeeding in his business, who was a taxpayer, and who possessed intelligence and high character, that individual was treated with the highest respect by the members of the white race. In proportion as we can multiply these examples, North and South, will our problem be solved."[73]

Washington wanted complete equality, but he believed that in the existing society, he could only do so much. He focused on what was possible, given the attitudes and beliefs of the times. He believed his work would help individuals arrive at an improved life now while laying a strong foundation for complete equality later.

Critics Emerge

As frustration grew, people began to criticize Washington. Decades had elapsed since slavery had ended, and African Americans had seen only small steps toward equality with white Americans. Washington charted a way to improved economic conditions, but once there, what was the next step? It was not surprising that a group arose demanding more than Washington offered.

Critics accused Washington of being too lenient in his demands for social integration and political rights. They said Washington had outlived his usefulness and his program placed blacks in a subservient position more like a new form of slavery than the promised land of equality. Now that the country was moving to a more industrial, mechanized economy, Washington's focus on farming and crafts seemed outmoded. Younger black activists born after the end of slavery burned with different goals than the man from Tuskegee.

Jim Crow

The name Jim Crow was applied to the hundreds of state and local laws that went into effect in the South to limit freedom for black residents. The name Jim Crow came from an 1820s entertainer, Thomas Rice, who while wearing blackface staged a minstrel show featuring the song, "Jump Jim Crow." The song presented an unflattering image of rural blacks, who according to the song wore torn clothes and danced like children. Eventually the many laws that established racial segregation became known as Jim Crow laws.

Most began appearing in the 1890s, as state legislatures passed laws that fashioned a segregated society in which whites retained the power, especially political, while blacks were consigned to an inferior status. Different states established different regulations. Alabama required separate waiting rooms and separate ticket windows for public transportation. Mississippi banned the promotion of equality of the races, and most southern states outlawed interracial marriages and integrated schools.

The Jim Crow system lasted in various forms until the 1960s, when the U.S. Congress passed laws prohibiting such practices.

A drawing of the Jim Crow character from a popular minstrel show of the early 1800s portrays a derogatory image of blacks as shabby and clownish.

Washington's continued insistence that African Americans focus on achieving economic equality by gaining practical skills such as furniture making, as these Tuskegee students are learning, gained him many critics, who thought his views were too soft on social and political issues.

Harsh attacks from prominent black leaders slowly gained steam after the turn of the century. The Reverend Charles Morris, a black New York minister, said on June 20, 1906, "I believe Booker T. Washington's heart is right, but that in fawning, cringing and groveling before the white man he has cost his race their rights and that twenty years hence, as he looks back and sees the harm his course has done to his race, he will be brokenhearted over it."[74]

John Hope, a professor at Atlanta Baptist College, thought Washington's statements gave people the idea that blacks did not want complete equality.

If we are not striving for equality, in heaven's name for what are we living? I regard it as cowardly and dishonest for any of our colored men to tell white people or colored people that we are not struggling for equality. If money, education, and honesty will not bring to me as much privilege, as much equality as they bring to any American citizen, then they are to me a curse, and not a blessing.[75]

One African American newspaper harshly concluded, "If there is anything in him except the most servile type of the old Negro we fail to find it."[76]

Washington's Response to Critics

Washington suffered most attacks in silence, concluding that some criticism was unavoidable. However, he answered the critics when he thought his program received unfair condemnation, especially from intellectuals he considered out of touch with reality and who "understand theories but they do not understand things. They know books but they do not know men. They know a great deal about the slavery controversy, for example, but they know almost nothing about the Negro. Especially are they igno-

1914 Speech

In 1914 Washington spoke to an Oklahoma gathering of the National Negro Business League. Despite the criticism that he had received over the past fifteen years, in this talk and others Washington doggedly stuck to his gospel of hard work.

Let your success thoroughly eclipse your shortcomings. We must give the world so much to think and talk about that relates to our constructive work in the direction of progress that people will forget and overlook our failures and shortcomings. Let us in the future spend less time talking about the part of the city that we cannot live in, and more time in making that part of the city that we can live in beautiful and attractive.

Quoted in Emmett J. Scott and Lyman Beecher Stowe, *Booker T. Washington: Builder of a Civilization.* Garden City, NY: Doubleday, Page, 1918, pp. 39–40.

rant in regard to the actual needs of the masses of colored people in the South today."[77]

Washington labeled his critics a group of newcomers who focused solely on the negative aspects of society rather than building on the successes following the Civil War. They wanted the nation's attention directed to the grievances of blacks and staged protests whenever possible to demand things that would take years to achieve. He suggested that moderation, not agitation, made more progress.

Washington was especially pointed in comparing his young critics with his life-long commitment to helping blacks.

> Any black man willing either in print or in public speech, to curse or abuse the white man, easily gained for himself a reputation for great courage. He might spend but thirty minutes or an hour once a year in that kind of "vindication" of his race, but he got the reputation of being an exceedingly brave man. Another man, who worked patiently and persistently for years in a Negro school, depriving himself of many of the comforts and necessities of life, in order to perform a service that would uplift his race, gained no reputation for courage. On the contrary, he was likely to be denounced as a coward by these "heroes," because he chose to do his work without cursing, without abuse, and without complaint.[78]

W.E.B. Du Bois

Washington found his most vocal antagonist in a man who at first promoted the Tuskegee agenda. W.E.B. Du Bois had praised Washington after the Atlanta speech for presenting a platform upon which whites and blacks could build a new order, but when little progress toward full equality transpired in the intervening years, he began to be critical. In 1903 Du Bois published a group of essays attacking Washington's program as impeding progress toward equality. Instead, Du Bois urged a more combative approach to the civil rights struggle. The two stood at polar ends from each other. Washington was the realist who put off full equality for a later day and concentrated on achievable goals, while Du Bois was the idealist who demanded everything now.

Washington's prime concern was for all of American society and how his people could best fit into it, whereas Du Bois cared little about how to fit in. He wanted equality now. Washington believed African Americans needed the support of white America, while Du Bois shunned white society as the enemy.

Du Bois tried to end Washington's dominance over black issues in the nation. He argued that the educator controlled where charity funds went, who was appointed to political office, and what message about civil rights was being fed to the nation. He accused Washington of selling out his race by making a deal with southern whites—a deal that required southern blacks to accept partial equality in return for improved economic opportunity. Du Bois mocked Washington's efforts, writing that white society adopted the attitude, "If that is all you and your race ask, take it."[79]

Du Bois hated to criticize a man he had admired, someone who had risen from slavery to heights attained by few men, black or white, yet felt he must if African Americans were to reach their true potential and rightful position.

> One hesitates, therefore, to criticize a life which, beginning with so little, has done so much. But so far as Mr. Washington apologises for injustice, North or South, does not rightly value the privilege and duty of voting, belittles the emasculating effects of caste distinctions, and opposes the higher training and ambition of our brighter minds—so far as he, the South, or the Nation does this—we must unceasingly and firmly oppose them.[80]

Du Bois accused Washington of yielding in three important areas—political power, civil rights, and higher education for African Americans. Without a fair opportunity in these arenas, Du Bois argued, how could black men and women attain equality? "Is it possible, and probable, that nine millions of men can make effective progress in economic lines if they are deprived of political rights, made a servile caste, and allowed only the most meager chance for developing their exceptional men?"

Du Bois contended that Washington's program led to "industrial slavery and civic death" and that it "practically accepts the alleged inferiority of the Negro races." He claimed that Washington promoted "a policy of submission" and that "manly self-

W.E.B. Du Bois aggressively challenged Washington's role as a spokesperson on the issues that faced African Americans and criticized his emphasis on promoting practical skills instead of advocating higher education and leadership as keys to achieving civil rights.

respect is worth more than lands and houses, and that a people who voluntarily surrender such respect, or cease striving for it, are not worth civilizing."[81]

Rather than building a better society on a foundation of farming and crafts, Du Bois believed that African Americans could be better guided through the efforts of what he called the Talented Tenth—the most educated 10 percent of the black population. Du Bois contended that education existed "not to make men

Although Washington's approach to achieving equality had its critics, he earned countless admirers for his work as an educator, leader, and promoter of issues important to African Americans.

carpenters," as he claimed Washington's work did, but "to make carpenters men."[82]

Du Bois claimed that Washington's notion of starting at the bottom and slowly working one's way upward had never worked in history and that black people needed the example and enlightenment of educated blacks to light the way. "The Talented Tenth of the Negro race must be made leaders of thought and missionaries of culture among their people. No others can do this work and Negro colleges must train men for it. The Negro race, like all other races, is going to be saved by its exceptional men."[83]

Trotter Incident

Agitation for equality increased as conditions worsened. Jim Crow legislation made it more difficult for blacks to attain real equality, and a startling rise in the number of lynchings in the South enraged Washington's opponents. The black publisher of the Boston, Massachusetts, newspaper, the *Guardian*, Monroe Trotter, published inflammatory articles and editorials calling for civil rights for African Americans and an end to racism.

Matters boiled over on July 30, 1903, when Washington arrived in Boston to deliver a speech before two thousand people, including Trotter. Boston police officers stood guard inside the auditorium in case a disturbance flared. The hostile crowd booed and hissed the first two speakers, who praised Washington's accomplishments. Apprehension rose when someone tossed a can of pepper onto the stage that caused the speakers to wheeze and cough.

When the master of ceremonies rose to introduce Washington, Trotter jumped from the audience and shouted insults. Trotter's supporters joined in, while Washington advocates hurled back their own biting comments. Heated words led to shoving, which in turn caused fistfights to break out.

Praise for an Educator

As one of the nation's most respected journalists, Ray Stannard Baker (1870–1946) observed the events and people of his day with astute perception. He came into contact with presidents, generals, financiers, and politicians, but few earned the praise he gave Booker T. Washington. He wrote these words about the Tuskegee educator in 1908.

> Nothing has been more remarkable in the recent history of the Negro than Washington's rise to influence as a leader, and the spread of his ideals of education and progress. The central idea of his doctrine is work. He teaches that if the Negro wins by real worth a strong economic position in the country, other rights and privileges will come to him naturally.
>
> He has brought new hope and given new courage to the masses of his race. He has given them a working plan of life. And is there a higher test of usefulness? Measured by any standard, white or black, Washington must be regarded today as one of the great men of this country: and in the future he will be so honored.

Ray Stannard Baker, "Following the Color Line," *American Magazine* (1908). www.spartacus.school net.co.uk/USAbooker.htm/5-6.

Boston police restored order before anyone was badly hurt, and in the aftermath they arrested Trotter. As they led Trotter away, Washington returned to the podium to deliver his speech.

Du Bois rarely agreed with Trotter's views, but his arrest enraged Du Bois. He believed that the black publisher had been exercising his constitutional right to freedom of speech and that the Boston police singled him out for arrest to placate Washington. "When Trotter went to jail, my indignation overflowed," wrote Du Bois. "I did not always agree with Trotter then or later. But he was an honest, brilliant, unselfish man, and to treat as a crime that which was at worse mistaken judgment was an outrage."[84]

Gathering of the Niagara Movement

The Trotter incident sparked Du Bois's desire to organize more aggressive efforts in behalf of African Americans. In the summer of 1905 he invited prominent African Americans from across the nation to gather at Niagara Falls, Canada. Twenty-nine men attended the first gathering, and the next year they issued a series of resolutions calling for equality. "We will not be satisfied to take one jot or tittle less than our full manhood rights. We claim for ourselves every single right that belongs to a freeborn American, political, civil, and social; and until we get these rights we will never cease to protest and assail the ears of America."[85]

The Niagara Movement proved to be a thorn in Washington's side for the rest of his life. As his final years arrived, Washington experienced a mixture of satisfaction at what he had accomplished and irritation that so many seemed to disagree with him.

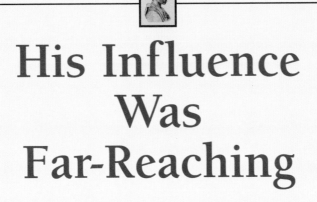

Chapter Seven

His Influence Was Far-Reaching

It seemed that Washington experienced more harsh criticism in the final ten years of his life and the years immediately after his death than in any other period. Certain events gave Washington's opponents more ammunition in their attacks against his philosophy. As the attacks gained momentum, the Tuskegee founder found it more and more difficult to battle them.

Race Riots

Two 1906 race riots led opponents to harshly censure Washington. A series of four alleged rapes in Atlanta produced four days of rioting that saw more than one hundred killed or wounded and many businesses, mostly black-owned, destroyed. Washington quickly canceled the rest of a New England trip to head to Atlanta. He urged the city's black citizens not to retaliate against the whites and to allow city authorities to restore order. Washington also met with prominent Atlanta leaders in hopes of improving race relations.

A pin urges support for the 167 African American troops of the Twenty-fifth Infantry, who were dishonorably discharged from the army in 1906 after a group of the soldiers who had resorted to violence sparked a series of racial incidents in Brownsville, Texas.

Du Bois, however, viewed the hostility as another sign that little progress could be made toward equality as long as people adhered to Washington's philosophy. Du Bois contended that southern whites had little desire to aid southern blacks and told black audiences to abandon the South and head north.

Later that year soldiers of the army's Twenty-fifth Infantry Regiment, a black unit stationed in Brownsville, Texas, battled with white residents following a series of racial incidents. In retaliation for previous assaults on black troops, a group of soldiers left camp and began firing randomly at homes of the white townspeople. They shot the horse of a mounted police officer who attempted to halt them, then marched to a saloon and killed the white barkeeper who had refused to serve them.

Though only a portion of the regiment participated, the unit's white commanding officer dismissed all 167 soldiers from service, including six men who had earned the Medal of Honor for courage under fire. Despite heated objections from Washington, President Roosevelt backed the army commander.

Even though Washington fought for the servicemen, Du Bois and other leaders of the Niagara Movement condemned Washington's association with the president and claimed he ignored current social evils. The Tuskegee leader emerged with a tarnished reputation.

Washington Takes a More Vigorous Approach

Even though Washington was often criticized for his public utterances and agendas, he had done much to advance the cause of African Americans. As early as the 1890s Washington had quietly battled certain ills. In 1898 he coauthored a letter to various state governments opposing southern states that placed strict requirements, such as a literacy test, on voting. Louisiana, for example, added a clause to its constitution stating that any male whose father or grandfather was qualified to vote on January 1, 1867, was automatically registered as a voter. If that were not the case, the man would have to take a test to qualify for voting. The law might appear fair, until one realizes that on January 1, 1867, all blacks in the South were slaves and unable to vote. So the law automatically excluded all blacks. Washington also penned a strong letter to newspapers condemning the alarming rise in the number of lynchings in the South, and without fanfare he financed some of the first legal cases against segregation.

He even came to the aid of his archrival Du Bois when a conductor on the Southern Railway refused to allow Du Bois to enter the sleeping car. Washington contacted Tuskegee trustee and railroad official William Henry Baldwin Jr. to remedy the situation, but his efforts made no headway in the racial climate of the time. With only a handful of people knowing, Washington sent money to Du Bois to help defray legal costs in the affair.

Washington became more public with his denunciation of racism in 1912 in an article in a prominent magazine. He argued that African Americans received an unfair deal in American society and faced disadvantages of which white America could hardly conceive. He particularly attacked discrimination in the education system, where one set of schools in the South existed for whites and another—less equipped and with substandard materials—for blacks. In speeches and other writings, Washington condemned segregated housing, travel, and inequality in courts of law, where blacks received harsher punishment than whites.

"If this country is to continue to be a Republic," he reminded audiences, "its task will never be completed as long as seven

Children stand outside a school for black students in Henderson County, Kentucky. Washington railed against the discrimination in the education system in the South, where black students attended schools with substandard materials and facilities compared with those available to white students.

or eight millions of its people are in a large degree regarded as aliens and are without voice or interest in the welfare of the Government."[86]

Washington continued that theme in 1913, when the nation celebrated the fiftieth anniversary of the end of slavery. Speaking to a large crowd gathered to mark the occasion, he claimed that the country had made progress in the percentage of African Americans that possessed their own land and homes, in the number who could read and write, and that racial relations had improved since the Civil War, yet much remained to be done. He said:

> It is just as true in America and in the South, as it is elsewhere, that a nation or a people cannot gain the highest success, even in a material sense, when one large portion of the population is so helpless and so inefficient as to be a burden, rather than a help, to the other portion. One portion of the community cannot be contented and happy when the other portion of the community is bitter, discontented and miserable.[87]

Another Speech Criticized

More race riots took place around the country. They seemed to prove Washington's point that much of American society remained discontent. Turbulent racial relations caused even more groups of African American leaders to call for improved conditions in education and more rights for all people. This led to the birth of the National Association for the Advancement of Colored People (NAACP) in 1908 and the Negro Urban League in 1911, two organizations that through the years helped advance conditions in business and in the community at large. The stance favoring a more aggressive approach to civil rights gained momentum in much of black America.

Washington ran headlong into this assertive spirit in 1910 when he addressed the Anti-Slavery and Aborigines Society in London, England. He painted a rosy image of American society, mentioning the areas of progress in racial relations while omitting any reference to lynchings, segregation, and other problems. Du Bois and twenty-two other prominent African Americans issued a statement condemning Washington's timid approach to race. They declared that any man, including someone as

A Harsh Condemnation

W.E.B. Du Bois and other African American leaders were bitterly disappointed with Washington's 1910 London, England, speech. They wished that he had been more severe in his condemnation of American society. In October 1910 Du Bois and twenty-two compatriots issued a signed statement expressing their views.

> The undersigned Negro-Americans have heard, with great regret, the recent attempt to assure England and Europe that their condition in America is satisfactory. They sincerely wish that such were the case, but it becomes their plain duty to say that [if] Mr. Booker T. Washington, or any other person, is giving the impression abroad that the Negro problem in America is in process of satisfactory solution, he is giving an impression which is not true.
>
> We say this without personal bitterness toward Mr. Washington. He is a distinguished American and has a perfect right to his opinions.
>
> Today in eight states where the bulk of the Negroes live, black men of property and university training can be, and usually are, by law denied the ballot, while the most ignorant white man votes.

Quoted in Spartacus Educational, "W.E.B. Du Bois." www.spartacus.schoolnet.co.uk/USAbooker.htm.

esteemed as Washington, who left the impression that all was well in society, was ignoring the facts and leaving an incorrect impression.

Washington reacted angrily to this attack on his judgment. He claimed that such criticism only pitted African American leaders against one another at a time when unity was important.

> When there is so much that is needed to be done in the way of punishing those who are guilty of lynching, of peonage, and seeing that the Negro gets an equitable share of the school fund, and that the law relating to the ballot is enforced in regard to black men and white men, it is difficult to see how people can throw away their time and strength in stirring up strife within the race.[88]

In March 1911 Washington sent a telegram to one of his adversaries in which he recommended that they all begin to work together. "I am convinced that the time has come when all interested in the welfare of the Negro people should lay aside personal differences and personal bickerings and anything and everything that smacks of selfishness and keep in mind only rendering the service which will best promote and protect the whole race in all of its larger interests."[89]

"What Are You Doing Here?"

That same month an assailant attacked Washington in New York as the educator walked the streets looking for a friend. Forty-year-old Henry Ulrich, a white resident, spotted Washington and

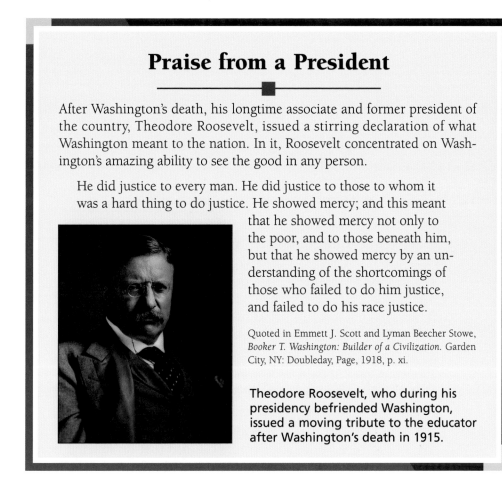

Praise from a President

After Washington's death, his longtime associate and former president of the country, Theodore Roosevelt, issued a stirring declaration of what Washington meant to the nation. In it, Roosevelt concentrated on Washington's amazing ability to see the good in any person.

> He did justice to every man. He did justice to those to whom it was a hard thing to do justice. He showed mercy; and this meant that he showed mercy not only to the poor, and to those beneath him, but that he showed mercy by an understanding of the shortcomings of those who failed to do him justice, and failed to do his race justice.

Quoted in Emmett J. Scott and Lyman Beecher Stowe, *Booker T. Washington: Builder of a Civilization.* Garden City, NY: Doubleday, Page, 1918, p. xi.

Theodore Roosevelt, who during his presidency befriended Washington, issued a moving tribute to the educator after Washington's death in 1915.

asked, "What are you doing here?" Ulrich had little idea who the black man was but was disturbed that an unfamiliar person, especially an African American, walked his neighborhood. Washington tried to explain his purpose, but Ulrich struck him five times on the side of his head. When Washington attempted to flee, Ulrich chased after him, cane in hand, and smacked Washington a dozen times as he ran. "If I'm breaking the law," uttered Washington, "call an officer and have him arrest me."[90]

A bloody Washington stumbled toward plainclothes policeman Chester Hagan who, thinking the black man was a thief, arrested the educator and took him to the nearest police station. Finally, Washington convinced them of his identity, and Lieutenant Robert Quinn dismissed the charges and placed Ulrich under arrest. Washington headed to a hospital, where a physician closed the wounds with sixteen stitches.

A jury later found Ulrich not guilty of any charges, but sympathy poured in for Washington. Roosevelt condemned Ulrich's actions, and Du Bois sent words of condolence. However, the affair did nothing to impede the demand for a more aggressive approach to civil rights.

Final Days

As always, when seeking refuge from the political battles and struggles for racial equality, Washington inevitably turned to Tuskegee. Despite the demands made on his time by forces that pulled him from the campus, Washington's true love was his school, where he could walk among his students and see the hopes for the future in their faces. Whenever he came back to campus, he was reinvigorated in only a day or two.

He had much of which to be proud. By 1915 more than two thousand students, impeccably dressed in crisp blue and white uniforms, attended classes held on 2,400 acres (971ha) of land, all neatly landscaped. Another two thousand students enrolled in extension classes held elsewhere. The highest praise came in the form of the many other schools throughout the South that tried to emulate what Washington had done at Tuskegee.

On October 25, 1915, Washington collapsed while on a speaking tour in New York City. Doctors claimed that he suffered from nervous exhaustion and arteriosclerosis and informed the educa-

Washington delivers an address at the Tuskegee Institute in 1915, not long before his death.

tor that he had only a short time left to live. Washington absorbed the bad news, then told assistants he wanted to return immediately to Tuskegee. He wanted to spend his final moments at the place that marked his career. "I was born in the South, I have lived and labored in the South, and I expect to die and be buried in the South,"[91] he said.

Washington arrived at Tuskegee late on November 13 after a long journey by train. The next morning, surrounded by family at his beloved Tuskegee, he died. The *Montgomery Advertiser* wrote that among the students on the campus as well as the town residents, "there is the feeling of personal loss. Nobody is hiding his tears. Nobody is free from gloom."[92]

Washington's body lay in state in the school's chapel for one day. Three days after his death Washington was buried in the small cemetery on campus. "He was the greatest Negro leader since Frederick Douglass and the most distinguished man, white or black, who has come out of the South since the Civil War," stated Du Bois. "His fame was international and his influence far-reaching. Of the good that he accomplished there can be no doubt; he directed the attention of the Negro race in America to the pressing necessity of economic development; he emphasized technical education and he did much to pave the way for an understanding between the white and darker races."[93]

His Legacy

Washington's death paved the way for bolder, more aggressive black leaders. They wasted little time pointing out the flaws in his agenda. They claimed that Washington looked to past practices and skills to help African Americans at a time when mass production and machines dominated industry and farming and that he focused on crafts more suited to the 1860s than to the twentieth century.

Supporters countered that one of Washington's most important talents was recognizing how far he could push his demands in a rigid southern society that placed him at a distinct disadvantage. They added that critics failed to see that Washington had no alternative. He was willing to take what he could get now, with the thought that more would follow later.

In a 1944 book examining race relations in the United States, Gordon Hancock, an African American professor of economics at Virginia Union University, concludes of Washington,

> The greatness of Booker T. Washington hinges about his common-sense approach to the question of race relations; and although his doctrines have been [criticized] by many who are unworthy to unlatch his shoes, his basic approach was sound. He reasoned that if the Negro could be made economically efficient he would stand a better chance of surviving even though his admittance to full citizenship be indefinitely postponed. This above all else marked the great wisdom and common sense that make Washington probably the greatest Negro in history.[94]

Other observers of Washington's career, looking back from many years in the future and thus enjoying the benefit of perspective, give Washington more credit than did his contemporaries. Noted historian John Hope Franklin, an African American who wrote a definitive history of African Americans in the United States, declared that Washington "was unquestionably the central figure—the dominant personality—in the history of Negro Americans down to his death in 1915. The vast majority of blacks acclaimed him as their leader, and few whites ventured into the matter of race relations without his counsel."[95] Franklin even titled the section of his history the "Age of Booker T. Washington."

A statue stands in tribute to the legacy of Booker T. Washington on the campus of what is now known as Tuskegee University.

A New Ship

■

During World War II the nation frequently paid tribute to its heroes by naming a ship in their honor. Booker T. Washington received such acclaim in 1942, when the sparkling freighter ship *Booker T. Washington* slid into the waters. The most significant fact was not that it bore an illustrious name but that it carried an integrated crew and was commanded by a black officer. *Time* magazine covered the ship's launching.

When the Liberty freighter *Booker T. Washington* goes into service, she will be commanded by a British West Indies–born Brooklyn man, the first Negro to hold a U.S. master's certificate. Captain [Hugh] Mulzac not only promised that he would be able to get qualified Negro officers to serve under him but said that he knew

white as well as Negro crewmen willing to serve under him—for the *Booker T.* is not to be a Jim Crow ship.

The *Booker T.* will serve not only in the war of ocean transport but in the war against race discrimination. [The] first Liberty ship to bear a Negro's name, she is the first to be christened by a member of the Negro race —Marian Anderson, contralto —and the first to heed a Negro's command.

Time, "The First Negro Skipper," October 5, 1942, p. 25.

Captain Hugh Mulzac commanded the Liberty freighter *Booker T. Washington* and its integrated crew when it was commissioned in 1942 during World War II.

The nation gradually gave honors to the educator. A ship was named in his honor during World War II, and a group of African American aviators who flew with distinction and bravery in the same war were called the Tuskegee airmen. In 1945 Washington became the first African American to be elected to the Hall of Fame of Great American.

Washington's legacy can be measured in the number of people, male and female, whose lives he touched. Thousands left Tuskegee with the skills needed to make a better place for themselves in society. They departed with a confidence instilled at Tuskegee, where they were exposed to Washington's philosophy and inspired by the success he had enjoyed.

Roy Wilkins, a top official in the NAACP, saw as much. In 1944 he stated:

> If it has seemed in the past that certain segments of the Negro population and certain leaders have demanded less than complete equality . . . closer study will show that the goal has always been complete equality. There is considerable evidence that that master politician on the race question, Booker T. Washington, carelessly nominated as the "half-loaf" leader, envisioned complete equality as the goal for his people. A shrewd man, thoroughly in tune with his time, he *appeared* to be an appeaser and did his great work under that protective cloak.[96]

Notes

Introduction: A Harvard Honor

1. Quoted in Louis R. Harlan, *Booker T. Washington: The Making of a Black Leader, 1856–1901*. New York: Oxford University Press, 1972, p. 235.

2. Booker T. Washington, *Up from Slavery*. New York: A.L. Burt, 1900, p. 296.

3. Quoted in B.F. Riley, *The Life and Times of Booker T. Washington*. New York: Fleming H. Revell, 1916, p. 219.

Chapter One: A Child in Slavery

4. Washington, *Up from Slavery*, p. 1.

5. Quoted in Harlan, *Booker T. Washington: The Making of a Black Leader*, p. 11.

6. Washington, *Up from Slavery*, p. 10.

7. Washington, *Up from Slavery*, p. 11.

8. Quoted in Harlan, *Booker T. Washington: The Making of a Black Leader*, p. 16.

9. Washington, *Up from Slavery*, p. 6.

10. Quoted in Harlan, *Booker T. Washington: The Making of a Black Leader*, p. 14.

11. Washington, *Up from Slavery*, p. 7.

12. Quoted in Harlan, *Booker T. Washington: The Making of a Black Leader*, p. 14.

13. Washington, *Up from Slavery*, p. 12.

14. Quoted in Basil Mathews, *Booker T. Washington: Educator and Inter-Racial Interpreter*. London: SCM Press, 1949, p. 19.

15. Washington, *Up from Slavery*, p. 15.

16. Washington, *Up from Slavery*, p. 19.

17. Washington, *Up from Slavery*, p. 21.

Chapter Two: On Fire with One Ambition

18. Washington, *Up from Slavery*, p. 27.

19. Washington, *Up from Slavery*, p. 28.

20. Washington, *Up from Slavery*, pp. 33–34.

21. Quoted in Mathews, *Booker T. Washington: Educator and Inter-Racial Interpreter*, pp. 40–41.

22. Washington, *Up from Slavery*, p. 39.

23. Quoted in Harlan, *Booker T. Washington: The Making of a Black Leader*, p. 42.

24. Washington, *Up from Slavery*, pp. 43–44.

25. Quoted in Harlan, *Booker T. Washington: The Making of a Black Leader*, p. 43.

26. Washington, *Up from Slavery*, pp. 40–41, 44.

27. Quoted in Harlan, *Booker T. Washington: The Making of a Black Leader*, p. 45.

28. Washington, *Up from Slavery*, pp. 42–43.

Chapter Three: "I Had Reached the Promised Land"

29. Quoted in Mathews, *Booker T. Washington: Educator and Inter-Racial Interpreter*, p. 47.

30. Washington, *Up from Slavery*, p. 51.

31. Quoted in Samuel R. Spencer Jr., *Booker T. Washington and the Negro's Place in American Life*. Boston: Little, Brown, 1955, p. 32.

32. Quoted in Harlan, *Booker T. Washington: The Making of a Black Leader*, p. 55.

33. Washington, *Up from Slavery*, p. 54.

34. Quoted in Riley, *The Life and Times of Booker T. Washington*, p. 71.

35. Washington, *Up from Slavery*, p. 57.

36. Quoted in Harlan, *Booker T. Washington: The Making of a Black Leader*, p. 76.

37. Quoted in Harlan, *Booker T. Washington: The Making of a Black Leader*, p. 66.

38. Quoted in Harlan, *Booker T. Washington: The Making of a Black Leader*, p. 83.

39. Washington, *Up from Slavery*, p. 88.

40. Washington, *Up from Slavery*, p. 104.

41. Quoted in Harlan, *Booker T. Washington: The Making of a Black Leader*, p. 91.

Chapter Four: "Making Bricks Without Straw"

42. Quoted in Mathews, *Booker T. Washington: Educator and Inter-Racial Interpreter*, p. 61.

43. Washington, *Up from Slavery*, p. 110.

44. Washington, *Up from Slavery*, p. 118.

45. Quoted in Harlan, *Booker T. Washington: The Making of a Black Leader*, p. 125.

46. Quoted in Spencer, *Booker T. Washington and the Negro's Place in American Life*, p. 61.

47. Washington, *Up from Slavery*, pp. 130–31.

48. Washington, *Up from Slavery*, p. 145.

49. Quoted in Spencer, *Booker T. Washington and the Negro's Place in American Life*, p. 51.

50. Washington, *Up from Slavery*, p. 208.

51. Quoted in John Hope Franklin, *From Slavery to Freedom: A History of Negro Americans*. New York: Knopf, 1974, p. 285.

52. Quoted in Emmett J. Scott and Lyman Beecher Stowe, Booker T. *Washington: Builder of a Civilization*. Garden City, NY: Doubleday, Page, 1918, p. xii.

53. Washington, *Up from Slavery*, p. 199.

54. Quoted in Spencer, *Booker T. Washington and the Negro's Place in American Life*, p. 95.

Chapter Five: "The Ascendancy of Mr. Booker T. Washington"

55. Quoted in Mathews, *Booker T. Washington: Educator and Inter-Racial Interpreter*, p. 83.

56. Quoted in Mathews, *Booker T. Washington: Educator and Inter-Racial Interpreter*, p. 84.

57. Washington, *Up from Slavery*, p. 213.

58. Washington, *Up from Slavery*, p. 220.

59. Quoted in Mathews, *Booker T. Washington: Educator and Inter-Racial Interpreter*, p. 89.

60. Washington, *Up from Slavery*, p. 221.

61. Washington, *Up from Slavery*, p. 222.

62. Washington, *Up from Slavery*, pp. 221–22.

63. Quoted in Rayford W. Logan, ed., *What the Negro Wants*. Chapel Hill: University of North Carolina Press, 1944, p. 54.

64. W.E.B. Du Bois, *The Souls of Black Folk*. New York: Gramercy Books, 1994, p. 33.

65. Washington, *Up from Slavery*, p. 255.

66. Quoted in Mathews, *Booker T. Washington: Educator and Inter-Racial Interpreter*, p. 99.

67. Washington, *Up from Slavery*, p. 300.

68. Quoted in Spencer, *Booker T. Washington and the Negro's Place in American Life*, p. 119.

69. Washington, *Up from Slavery*, p. 276.

70. Quoted in C. Vann Woodward, *Origins of the New South, 1877–1913*. Baton Rouge: Louisiana State University Press, 1951, p. 465.

71. Quoted in Edmund Morris, *Theodore Rex*. New York: Random House, 2001, p. 54.

72. Quoted in H.W. Brands, *T.R.: The Last Romantic*. New York: Basic Books, 1997, p. 423.

Chapter Six: "To Make Carpenters Men"

73. Quoted in Mathews, *Booker T. Washington: Educator and Inter-Racial Interpreter*, p. 184.

74. Quoted in Mathews, *Booker T. Washington: Educator and Inter-Racial Interpreter*, p. 283.

75. Quoted in Page Smith, *The Rise of Industrial America*. New York: McGraw-Hill, 1984, p. 62.

76. Quoted in Mark Bauerlein, "Washington, Du Bois, and the Black Future," *Wilson Quarterly*, Autumn 2004, p. 1.

77. Quoted in Spencer, *Booker T. Washington and the Negro's Place in American Life*, p. 140.

78. Quoted in Mathews, *Booker T. Washington: Educator and Inter-Racial Interpreter*, p. 293.

79. W.E.B. Du Bois, *The Souls of Black Folk*. New York: p. 36.

80. Quoted in Mathews, *Booker T. Washington: Educator and Inter-Racial Interpreter*, p. 280.

81. Du Bois, *The Souls of Black Folk*, pp. 40–43.

82. Quoted in Spencer, *Booker T. Washington and the Negro's Place in American Life*, pp. 155–56.

83. Quoted in Spencer, *Booker T. Washington and the Negro's Place in American Life*, pp. 155–56.

84. W.E.B. Du Bois, *Dusk of Dawn*. New York: Schocken, 1968, pp. 87–88.

85. Quoted in Du Bois, *Dusk of Dawn*, p. 90.

Chapter Seven: His Influence Was Far-Reaching

86. Quoted in Mathews, *Booker T. Washington: Educator and Inter-Racial Interpreter*, pp. 210–11.

87. Quoted in Mathews, *Booker T. Washington: Educator and Inter-Racial Interpreter*, p. 211.

88. Quoted in Spencer, *Booker T. Washington and the Negro's Place in American Life*, p. 176.

89. Quoted in Mathews, *Booker T. Washington: Educator and Inter-Racial Interpreter*, p. 292.

90. Quoted in Louis R. Harlan, *Booker T. Washington: The Wizard of Tuskegee, 1901–1915*. New York: Oxford University Press, 1983, pp. 380–81.

91. Quoted in Spencer, *Booker T. Washington and the Negro's Place in American Life*, p. 194.

92. Quoted in Harlan, *Booker T. Washington: The Wizard of Tuskegee*, p. 455.

93. Du Bois, *Dusk of Dawn*, p. 242.

94. Quoted in Logan, *What the Negro Wants*, p. 222.

95. Franklin, *From Slavery to Freedom*, p. 290.

96. Quoted in Logan, *What the Negro Wants*, pp. 116–17.

For More Information

Books

H.W. Brands, *T.R.: The Last Romantic*. New York: Basic Books, 1997. Brands offers one of the most readable and thorough biographies of Theodore Roosevelt available. He includes a fine section dealing with the racial issue and Washington's dinner with Roosevelt at the White House.

W.E.B. Du Bois, *Dusk of Dawn*. New York: Schocken, 1968. Du Bois's autobiography ranks in importance with that of Washington. Du Bois shows how events fashioned his views and explains his experiences as an African American.

————, *The Souls of Black Folk*. New York: Gramercy, 1994. This collection of essays gained Du Bois immense renown. His chapter pertaining to Washington's influence is still a classic presentation of how the two leaders disagreed.

Louis R. Harlan, *Booker T. Washington: The Making of a Black Leader, 1856–1901*. New York: Oxford University Press, 1972. Harlan's two volumes on Washington are easily the best study of Washington yet produced. Written in a very readable style, the book offers a fascinating look at the educator's life and career. This volume covers the period from Washington's birth until shortly after becoming nationally renowned.

————, *Booker T. Washington: The Wizard of Tuskegee, 1901–1915*. New York: Oxford University Press, 1983. Volume two of Harlan's stellar biography covers the last fourteen years of Washington's life. Like the first volume, this book quickly draws the reader's attention.

Stephen Mansfield, *Then Darkness Fled: The Liberating Wisdom of Booker T. Washington*. Nashville: Cumberland House, 2002. Mansfield's thorough research produces a fine biography of Washington. More suitable for high school students, the book points out the principles that guided the educator's career.

Patricia and Frederick McKissack, *Booker T. Washington: Leader and Educator*. Berkeley Heights, NJ: Enslow, 1992. Focusing on junior high school students, the McKissacks offer an examination of Washington's entire life. This is an excellent place to start for students.

Anne E. Schraff, *Booker T. Washington: Character Is Power*. Berkeley Heights, NJ: Enslow, 2006. Geared for middle school students, Schraff points out the motivating factors behind Washington's career.

Alan Schroeder and Anne Beier, *Booker T. Washington: Educator and Racial Spokesman*. Philadelphia: Chelsea House, 2005. Schroeder and Beier offer one of the most comprehensive biographies of Washington's life. Excellent for junior high or high school students.

Samuel R. Spencer Jr., *Booker T. Washington and the Negro's Place in American Life*. Boston: Little, Brown, 1955. Spencer's brief volume remains one of the finest places to begin a study of Washington's life.

Gwenyth Swain, *A Hunger for Learning: A Story About Booker T. Washington*. Minneapolis: Lerner, 2005. A part of the publisher's Creative Minds Biographies series for elementary students, Swain writes a readable account of Washington's life.

Booker T. Washington, *Up from Slavery*. New York: A.L. Burt, 1900. One cannot understand Washington without reading his influential autobiography. He depicts the agonizing and the heartwarming moments with equal freshness and uses the book to promote his philosophy on advancement.

C. Vann Woodward, *Origins of the New South, 1877–1913*. Baton Rouge: Louisiana State University Press, 1951. Woodward, one of the most prominent historians dealing with the South, contributes a thorough study here of racial relations while Washington lived.

Recordings

Booker T. Washington, *Atlanta Exposition Address*. Smithsonian Folkways Recordings, 1977. Listen to the speech that made Washington a national figure. Available to download at Amazon.com.

Web Sites

The Booker T. Washington Papers (www.historycooperative.org/btw/index.html). This Web site contains many of Washington's writings, including his autobiography and his letters, all available for downloading. The site also offers numerous photographs and links to other Web sites.

Documents in the American South (http://docsouth.unc.edu/fpn/washington/menu.html). This Web site offers for downloading not only Washington's autobiography but other key writings and documents relating to the African American experience in the United States.

Hampton University (www.hamptonu.edu). This Web site offers a summary of the current programs offered at the institution today, as well as information on its origins and contributions to society.

National Archives and Records Administration: "The Emancipation Proclamation" (www.archives.gov/exhibits/featured_documents/emancipation_proclamation). A vast collection of material exists at this government Web site, including the important documents from American history.

National Park Service: "Booker T. Washington" (www.nps.gov/bowa/index.htm). This government Web site includes basic information on Washington and about the Booker T. Washington National Monument at Hardy, Virginia.

Spartacus Educational (www.spartacus.schoolnet.co.uk/USAbooker.htm). A general Web site containing a brief biography of Washington as well as quotes by the man and individuals who knew him.

Tuskegee University (www.tuskegee.edu). The Web site for Washington's famous school contains information on the institution's history, qualifications for admission, and its current role in educating students.

Index

Picture Credits

Cover: © Corbis
AP Images, 69, 98
© Bettmann/Corbis, 15, 24, 25, 47, 51, 79, 95, 97
© Gary W. Carter/Corbis, 13
© Corbis, 29, 36, 50, 54, 72
© David J. & Janice L. Frent Collection/Corbis, 73, 88
Hulton Archive/Getty Images, 9, 31, 70
The Library of Congress, 10, 21, 33, 38, 44, 56, 65, 78, 83, 84, 90
MPI/Getty Images, 61
Stock Montage/Getty Images, 93
© Underwood & Underwood/Corbis, 67
© Jim West/The Image Works, 59

About the Author

John F. Wukovits is a retired junior high school teacher and writer from Trenton, Michigan, who specializes in history and biography. Besides biographies of Anne Frank, Jim Carrey, Michael J. Fox, Stephen King, and Martin Luther King Jr. for Lucent, he has written biographies of the World War II commander Admiral Clifton Sprague, Barry Sanders, Tim Allen, Jack Nicklaus, Vince Lombardi, and Wyatt Earp. He is also the author of many books about World War II, including the July 2003 book *Pacific Alamo: The Battle for Wake Island*, the August 2006 *One Square Mile of Hell: The Battle for Tarawa*, and the November 2006 *Eisenhower: A Biography*. A graduate of the University of Notre Dame, Wukovits is the father of three daughters—Amy, Julie, and Karen—and the grandfather of Matthew, Megan, Emma, and Kaitlyn.